CW00557218

THE
LITTLE
BOOK
OF
NORWICH

NEIL R. STOREY

The
History
Press

For Sarah

First published 2015
Reprinted 2017

The History Press
The Mill, Brimscombe Port
Stroud, Gloucestershire, GL5 2QG
www.thehistorypress.co.uk

British Library Cataloguing in Publication Data.
A catalogue record for this book is available from the British Library.

ISBN 978 0 7509 6142 4

Typesetting and origination by The History Press
Printed and bound by TJ International, Padstow, Cornwall.

Cover image: istock 4591133

CONTENTS

INTRODUCTION

'What a grand, higgledy-piggledy, sensible old place Norwich is.'
J.B. Priestley

Norwich, located in the far east of England, is a historic and, in many places, a green and beautiful city. It is the county town of Norfolk but remains distinct from the rest of the region, with its own local government, markets, festivals, dialect, music and culture, and there was even a time when it had its own law courts, prison and police force.

This book does not pretend to be a history, concise almanac or even a guide to Norwich; instead it is a collection of ephemeral, nostalgic and miscellaneous facts about a city brimming with history and full of fascinating stories. The contents of this volume will enliven a conversation or quiz, reveal the truths behind local myths and legends, and leave even those who know the city with the 'well fancy that!' factor. It will answer such burning questions as:

- What does a whiffler do?
- How tall is the spire of Norwich Cathedral?
- Who was Billy Bluelight?
- What connections do Mary Berry, David Frost, Muhammad Ali, Reg Kray and Philip Pullman have with the city?
- Where did Norwich City Football Club play its first matches?
- When did Norwich have a camouflage school?
- … and what, exactly, does Tombland mean?

Enquire within for the answers and a whole lot more to help you impress and intrigue friends, and confound even the most knowledgeable of Norwich citizens. Read this book from cover to cover or dip into it as you please – there are no rules – but above all, enjoy it.

Neil R. Storey, 2015

1

ABOUT
THE CITY

NORWICH IS BORN

Archaeological finds, dating back to the eighth century AD, were discovered in Fishergate and suggest that the first settlement that could be thought of as Norwich – known then as Northwic or Norvic – existed there.

The first definite record of the place name Norvic appears on coins minted between AD 920 and AD 939 during the reign of King Athelstan of England.

Norwich would become a city in 1194, during the reign of Richard I.

NORWICH HAMLETS

The old hamlets within the county of the City of Norwich were places where the inhabitants were entitled to the same municipal privileges as those residing within the walls of the city, namely Earlham, Eaton, Heigham, Hellesdon, Lakenham, Pockthorpe, Thorpe, Trowse Millgate, Old Catton and Sprowston.

TOMBLAND

Tombland does not refer to a burial ground. The first syllable comes from the Old English *tom*, meaning empty or open, thus Tombland means empty or open space – exactly what was needed to accommodate the market that was regularly here during the late Saxon period.

NORWICH CASTLE

Construction of Norwich Castle started shortly after the Norman Conquest of 1066. An area of land was cleared, defensive ditches were dug and a wooden fort was erected. In 1094, the reign of King William Rufus saw work begin on a stone keep and, after Rufus' death, his brother Henry I continued with the construction. The castle was completed by 1121.

Designed more as a symbol of power than as a necessary fortification, it is possible that the castle was intended to serve as a royal residence, although no Norman king ever lived there. In fact, it has spent the majority of its existence as the county gaol, a role it served from the fourteenth century until 1887, when the last prisoners were removed to a new prison off Plumstead Road and work began to convert the ancient castle into a museum which was opened in 1894.

GROWTH OF THE CITY

The old boundaries of the City of Norwich spread between St Clement's Hill in the north to Harford Bridge in the south, a distance of 4.25 miles. Following a zigzag boundary, it was around 17 miles in circumference and comprised 6,630 acres of land.

In 1066, Norwich was one of the largest towns in England, with an Anglo-Dutch population of around 5,500.

In 1377, a census taken of some of the great towns of England recorded that Norwich contained 5,300 people.

By the sixteenth century, Norwich had grown to become the second-largest city in England and continued to vie with Bristol as the 'second city' of England until the Industrial Revolution.

OLDEST SITES

The oldest dwelling place in Norwich is the Music House on King Street, which was built in about 1175 by the Jurnets, one of the wealthiest Jewish families in England. It became known as the Music House after its time as the headquarters for the Norwich waits and minstrels during the reign of Elizabeth I.

The oldest surviving pub in the city is the Adam and Eve in Bishopsgate. It was built in 1249 as a brewhouse for the workers building the cathedral.

The oldest remaining bridge in Norwich is the medieval Bishop Bridge, built in 1295.

BRIDGING THE GAP

By 1300 there were five bridges over the Wensum in Norwich, making it the city with the most bridges in England.

CITY WALLS

The city walls were started in 1294 and took around fifty years to complete due to complaints about the cost being levied for their construction. In the end they were completed by a single patriotic individual, Norwich tradesman Richard Spynk, who in 1343 was rewarded by the grateful Corporation by being 'quit all tallages, tasks and costs' for both he and his heirs forever. Once completed the walls had twelve gates, they were:

- Ber Street Gate, taken down in 1807
- Bishop's Gate, taken down in 1791
- Brazen Doors or Newgate, taken down in 1793
- Conisford Gate, at the south end of King Street, taken down in 1793
- Heigham Gate or Hell Gate, fell down in the eighteenth century
- Magdalen Gate, taken down in 1808

- Pockthorpe Gate, taken down in 1792
- St Augustine's Gate, taken down in 1794
- St Giles' Gate, taken down in 1792
- St Martin's or Coslany Gate, taken down in 1793
- St Stephen's or Nedham Gate, taken down in 1793
- Westwick or St Benedict's Gate, taken down in 1793

CHAPEL FIELD GARDENS

The Field takes its name from the chapel of St Mary in the Fields. Founded in the thirteenth century by John le Brun, St Mary in the Fields had such numerous and generous benefactors that it soon became a college, complete with a dean, chancellor, precentor, treasurer and seven other prebendaries, and the premises were expanded. At the time of the Dissolution, the extensive premises were granted to Miles Spencer LL.D, the last dean. The 'chapel' stood on the site of today's Assembly Rooms.

In 1406, the citizens of Norwich claimed 4.5 acres of ground that belonged to the Chapel in the Field. During the sixteenth century, what was know as Chapel Field was leased, complete with cherry yard and dove house, to notable citizens. Then, under a proclamation of 1578, it was used as an open area for mustering the trained bands, archers or the artillery and the 'fit place' to charge guns with shot and powder for the exercise of shooting. It was also the place where the 'City Tent' was set up for the Lord Lieutenant on the occasions of the general musters and where yearly reviews of the city regiment took place in the seventeenth century.

Chapel Field was first railed with fencing in 1707 and tree planting began when Sir Thomas Churchman leased The Field and laid out the main walks in 1746. In 1792, part of The Field was leased to become a large water reservoir for the city. Standing around 300yds in circumference with a high red-brick crenated water tower, it served this purpose until 1851 when the new Waterworks Company was established and reservoirs were built at Lakenham. In 1854, the old water basin was filled in and the people of the city lost a popular spot for skating. The Field then declined into a rough and uncared for place where washerwomen hung out their linen, children played and sheep were occasionally put out to graze.

After the Norfolk Agricultural Association held its annual meeting on The Field, attempts to improve it were made and new iron palisadings were erected in 1866 when their Royal Highnesses, the Prince and Princess of Wales, accompanied by the Queen of Denmark, were received there. But it was over ten years later, in 1877, that the Corporation realised that the shabby field could be made into a beauty spot and the landscape gardener got to work. The newly laid out gardens were opened by the mayor, Harry Bullard, with much festivity in 1880. The cost of the complete transformation was about £1,400.

GUILDHALL

The flint Guildhall was built between 1407 and 1413, and when complete it was the largest and most elaborate city hall outside London.

It primarily functioned as a place for meetings of the city's council, but gets its name from the Guild of St George who also used the building. The Guildhall remained the seat of the city council until it was replaced by City Hall in 1938.

The Guildhall once had a tower, built in 1435, but it collapsed in 1511 and was never rebuilt.

NORWICH MARKETS

The ancient trading rows and markets of Norwich (listed before the reign of Richard II) consisted of Glover's Row, Mercer's Row, Spicer's Row, Needler's Row, Tawer's Row, Ironmoner's Row, the Apothecary's Market, the Herb Market, the Poultry Market, the Bread Market, the Flesh Market, the Wool and Sheep Market, the Fish Market, the Hay Market, the Wood Market, the Cheese Market, the Leather Market, the Cloth-cutter's Market and the White-ware Market.

The Market Cross that once stood in the Market Place was constructed between 1501–03 by Mayor John Rightwise. A commodious and handsome building, it stood for over 200 years until it fell into decay. In 1732 it was sold by the Tonnage Committee for £125 and was taken down soon after.

THE CITY'S COAT OF ARMS

The city's arms consist of a ruby shield featuring a triple-towered castle in pearl above a royal lion, a symbol that was granted to the city by Edward III. The blazon of the arms is: 'Gules, a castle triple-towered and domed Argent; in base a lion passant guardant Or.'

This design appeared on a fifteenth-century seal and was confirmed during a heraldic visitation in 1562 by William Harvey, Clarenceux King of Arms. The arms are supported by two angels with their wings expanded (not included in the image below) and is surmounted by a fur winter cap of maintenance as its crest. The lower part was often shown embellished with sword and maces. The earliest depiction of the arms, including additions, to survive is in the form of a carving, was created in around 1534 and built into the outside wall of the Guildhall.

NEAR MISS FOR PULL'S FERRY

The picturesque fifteenth-century riverside watergate, Pull's Ferry, is today one of the city's most famous landmarks. It was, however, very nearly lost forever.

The watergate is named after John Pull, who ran the ferry across the Wensum from 1796 to 1841. It continued to operate until the 1930s (its last full year of operation being 1929), but after a number of years of disuse it became derelict and dilapidated. The structure was only saved after the Girl Guides lost their old local headquarters in an air raid during the Second World War. They subsequently raised and were given grants to the value of £2,000 to restore the historic building as their new headquarters in 1949.

IT'S PLAIN TO SEE

One of many reasons why Norwich is distinctive from other cities is its number of 'plains' – local dialect for an open space or square in the city. The word is derived from the Dutch and Flemish settlers who came to the city in the sixteenth century and used the word *plein* to describe such places.

THE POPULATION OF NORWICH SINCE 1693

1693	29,911	1921	112,533
1752	36,369	1931	126,207
1786	40,061	1941	112,669
1801	35,633	1951	110,633
1821	50,173	1961	116,231
1841	60,418	1971	122,118
1861	74,414	1981	119,764
1881	79,977	1991	127,074
1891	100,964	2001	121,553
1901	100,815	2011	132,512
1911	121,493		

A HOLE IN THE KING'S HEAD

In 1813, Alderman Jonathan Davey shocked the Guildhall Council Chamber by declaring, 'Gentlemen, I mean to put a hole in the King's Head!' His refusal to withdraw or explain his comment caused such great concern that local constables were ordered to observe his movements. The following week, an inn was sold on The Walk and the next day a huge hole appeared in the facade of the King's Head pub. It was turned into a shopper's foot street and, to this day, Davey Place remains a testimony to his sense of humour or perhaps his flair for publicity.

THE CORN HALL

The first brick of the new Norwich Corn Hall, otherwise known as the Corn Exchange, was laid on 1 May 1861 and opened for business on 9 November that same year. The contractors for the building were Messrs Ling and Balls of Norwich, and Messrs Barnard, Bishop, and Barnard for the roof. The total cost was about £8,000 and the work was executed from the designs of Mr Barry, of Norwich, and Mr H. Butcher, of No. 37 Bedford Row, London. It was used for public events, entertainments and sporting matches such as boxing and wrestling, but sadly it was demolished in 1964.

THE LOST PAGODA

There was once a fine ornamented pavilion or pagoda that stood near the centre of Chapel Field. Designed by Thomas Jeckyll of London, it was made by Messrs Barnard, Bishop and Barnard in cast and wrought iron at their Norfolk Ironworks in the city. It originally cost £2,000, weighed 40 tons, measured 35ft long by 18ft wide and stood 35ft high with two floors, the upper of which was reached by a spiral staircase. The pagoda was used as a showpiece for various exhibitions, the first being at the Philadelphia Centennial Exhibition in 1876, and at exhibitions in Paris, Vienna, Buenos Aires and London before the Norwich Corporation bought it in 1880 for the nominal sum of £250, another £250 being required for foundations, erection and painting. It was erected the following year and the first band played there on 24 May 1881. The pagoda stood on Chapel Field through the two world wars, when it could well have been lost to scrap salvage. It was eventually declared 'unsafe' and taken down in 1949.

LOST LANDMARK

One of the features that stood out on arrival into Norwich from the late nineteenth and well into the twentieth century, was the Boileau drinking fountain for horses and their drivers at the junction of Newmarket and Ipswich Roads. Sir John Boileau had bequeathed the sum of £1,000 to pay for the fountain in memory of his wife, Lady Catherine.

Designed by Thomas Jeckyll of London, Sir Joseph Boehm executed the statuary – entitled *Charity* – in bronze, while the tall uprights and the canopy were constructed by Mr Hubbard of East Dereham. It was inaugurated on 30 October 1876 and Sir Francis Boileau performed the ceremony of asking the city to accept the fountain before being thanked by the mayor, Mr J.H. Tillett, in the name of the citizens. After being declared unstable, the structure was taken down in 1965 and the statue moved a short distance away. Today it stands in the redeveloped grounds of the old Norfolk and Norwich Hospital.

A TERRIBLE DAY

The most serious and destructive fire to take place in Norwich during the nineteenth century occurred on 1 August 1898. At an early hour in the morning, the premises of Daniel Hurn, a rope maker who lived on Dove Street, were found on fire. The flames spread southwards to Messrs Chamberlin and Sons' wholesale warehouse, northwards towards Pottergate Street and westward to the public library. The premises in which the fire originated, the warehouse, and a portion of the property on the north were all speedily destroyed, and ultimately the main library building was consumed along with its 60,000 volumes and the valuable Norton Library.

By some terrible coincidence, Norwich Central Library caught fire almost 100 years later on 1 August 1994, with extensive damage caused. It was also on 1 August – this time in 1970 – that the popular department store Garlands, on London Street, was discovered on fire.

COURTS AND YARDS

In 1900, there were 749 courts and yards in Norwich, many of which have since disappeared through slum clearance, bombing during the war years and redevelopment. Here is a nostalgic list of some of them; many were named after the pubs that they once served:

Bath House Yard, Oak Street
Bird-in-Hand Yard, Barrack Street
Boarded Entry Yard, Ber Street
Cardinal's Cap Yard, St Benedict's Street
Cattermoul's Yard, Pitt Street
Cock and Pie Yard, Quayside
Cock Yard, St Giles Street
Crawfoot's Yard, Ber Street
Crown Court Yard, Elm Hill
Flower-in-Hand Yard, Heigham Street
Gaffer's Yard, St Benedict's Street
Greenland Fishery Yard, Oak Street
Grimmer's Court, St Andrew's Broad Street
Little Cow Yard, Cow Hill
Loyalty Court, St Stephen's Street
Museum Court, St Andrew's Broad Street
Oby's Yard, King Street
Pipe Burner's Yard, Pottergate Street
Ratcatcher's Yard, Ber Street
Rock Yard, Barrack Street
Seven Stars Yard, Barrack Street
Sultzer's Court, Botolph Street
Thoroughfare Yard, Magdalen Street
Tiger Yard, Fishgate Street
Two Quarts Court, Bridge Street
Wrestler's Yard, Barrack Street

SOME UNUSUAL STREET NAMES IN NORWICH PAST

Winkle's Row, King Street
Bull Close Road
St Laurence Little Steps, St Benedict's Street
Back of the Inns
Cockey Lane (now London Street)
Gropekunte Lane (now Opie Street)
Curson's Opening, Philadelphia Lane
Pig Lane, Palace Street
Rampant Horse Street
Weed's Square, Bishop's Bridge Road
Hangman's Lane (now Heigham Street)
Fuller's Hole, St Martin's Road

World's End Lane
Upper Goat Lane
Twenty-One Row (New Lakenham)
Zipfel's Court, Magdalen Street
Mountergate

LAST AND FIRST

The last Mayor of Norwich was the antiquarian Walter Rye
who served 1908–09. The title then changed to Lord Mayor and
Dr E.E. Blyth was the first to take this post that same year (1909–10).
Rye always maintained: 'The old plain Mayoralty of Norwich was
more honourable than a later-given Lord Mayorship.'

DEATH BELL NELLIE

When the mighty bell of the clock atop the 206ft tower of City Hall
was heard sonorously striking the hours for the first time in 1938,
it was dubbed 'Death Bell Nellie' – it is thought to be one of the
deepest-sounding clock bells in the country and it is certainly
the largest. For some, City Hall has never had much aesthetic
appeal. When Norman Long, a popular comedian of the day,
lampooned City Hall as a 'marmalade factory' during a show at the
Norwich Hippodrome, the nom de plume stuck for years after.

City Hall also has the longest balcony in England, at 365ft long (111m). It was suggested among the people of Norwich that the City Hall, which remained remarkably unscathed through the blitz on the city during the Second World War, had been deliberately missed on the orders of the Führer himself as he wanted the building intact so it could become his headquarters in the east.

CASTLE MALL

The Castle Mall shopping complex, completed in September 1993, cost £75 million to construct as part of a £145 million redevelopment project of the old Cattle Market site. The cast-iron arch erected over the entrance to the Castle Mall car park once spanned the River Wensum as part of the Duke's Palace Bridge from 1822 until it was replaced by the new bridge in 1972.

TWINNINGS

Norwich is twinned with four towns and cities:

- Rouen, France, since 1951
- Koblenz, Germany, since 1978
- Novi Sad, Serbia, since 1985
- El Viejo, Nicaragua, since 1996

NORWICH AROUND THE WORLD

There are seven places named Norwich in the USA, they appear in Connecticut, Kansas and Long Island, there are two in New York State, and two more in Vermont. There is also a Norwich in Ontario, Canada.

SOME MORE NORWICH FACTS

Norwich is the most easterly city in the United Kingdom.

It is latitude 52°42' north and longitude 1°20' east of Greenwich.

An ancient saying states that Norwich has 'a pub for every day of the year and a church for every week' – if the Nonconformist churches and chapels are counted then this still holds true, as does the number of pubs.

In 1404, the citizens of Norwich obtained a charter from Henry IV for its first mayor and two sheriffs to be appointed.

In 1509, a fire swept through the city and destroyed 718 houses. The City Corporation subsequently decreed that no newly erected buildings would be roofed with thatch.

The 'cross' on Boundary Road (near ASDA) was first erected in the fifteenth century to mark the spot where the King's Way crossed the boundary of the City of Norwich.

In 1712, an Act was passed for the illumination of the streets of Norwich, whereby, as soon as it got dark, every householder would hang lamps or candles outside their houses until 11 p.m.

The names of the streets and highways of the city were affixed to walls and displayed for the first time on 1 March 1771.

The moat surrounding the Castle Hill and the ascent from thence were laid out as gardens and shrubberies in 1784.

The clocks of Norwich were regulated upon Greenwich mean time as early as 1794.

The first gaslight was installed in Norwich on 21 December 1814, in Mr Harrison's hosiery shop in the Market Place.

The beautifully carved Bassingham Gate – formerly the entrance to the house of Tudor goldsmith John Bassingham at Nos 57–59 London Street – was bought by William Wilde when London Street was widened in the mid-1850s. In 1857 it was installed at the magistrate's entrance at the south-west corner of the Guildhall.

The first record of a telephone wire erected in Norwich was in December 1881 when the United Telephone Company suspended a line of wire between Messrs Morgan's Brewery, King Street and Mousehold House, the residence of the head brewer, Mr William H. Hackblock.

The wettest year in Norwich was 1912. A total of 40.74in of rain fell on the city and the heavy rainfall caused serious flooding.

In 1928, water mains formed from tree trunks were unearthed in King Street. This discovery indicates that some form of piped water system existed in at least one part the city as early as the fifteenth century.

Postcodes were introduced in Norwich in 1959.

During the coypu epidemic and cull of the 1970s, there was a Ministry of Agriculture Coypu Research Laboratory in Norwich.

In 2011, a news story revealed that Norwich has the shortest set of double yellow lines in Britain. Painted on the road surface of Stafford Street, they measure just 17in (41cm). Incredibly, this claim was beaten in 2013 in Cambridge, I bet locals were left wondering what vehicle you could fit in to that space if you were allowed to park there.

Norwich was designated England's first UNESCO (United Nations Educational, Scientific and Cultural Organisation) City of Literature in May 2012.

2

UPRISINGS, THE MILITARY AND WAR

RIOT AND REVOLT

The citizens of Norwich did not always get on with the servants of the cathedral priory. There were violent exchanges on a number of occasions, but one day those old animosities boiled over into a full-blown riot. During a fair held on Tombland in June 1272, an argument broke out and a mob of citizens drove a group of priory men back to the cathedral close. As the priory men were being forced back, one of them – armed with a crossbow – shot and killed a citizen. Days and weeks passed, and the citizens of Norwich were outraged that no action was taken in consequence for the man's death. As a result, an attack was launched against the cathedral and Bartholomew Cotton's *Historia Anglicana* provides an account:

> 1272, on the day following the Feast of St Laurence, the citizens of Norwich laid siege around the precincts of the monastery. When their insults failed to gain them admittance, they set fire to the main gate into the monastery ... they burned the dormitory, the refectory, the guest hall, the infirmary with its chapel and indeed almost all the buildings within the precincts of the monastery. They killed many members of the monastery's household, some sub deacons and clerics and some lay people in the cloister and in the monastery. Others they dragged off and put to death in the city.

After the fire, the citizens entered the buildings and looted everything the flames had spared; sacred vessels and books were taken, as well as gold and silver. In the immediate aftermath, King Henry III arrived to personally ensure that justice would be done to the 'delinquent citizens'. Alleged participants and ringleaders of the riot were tried and thirty of them were found guilty. Those condemned were dragged to the gallows by horses, hanged, then cut down and their bodies were burned to ashes. Keen to dissuade the citizens of Norwich from further outbursts of this nature, Henry III also deprived the citizens of their liberties. The Pope then laid Norwich under an interdict and called for the city to pay a large fine and build the Ethelbert Gate as penance.

PEASANT'S REVOLT, 1381

Across England, peasants rose up in protest against the oppressive nature of the Poll Tax. In June 1381, Geoffrey 'John' Litster (also spelt Litester), a dyer of some means from Felmingham, led a rising in the north-eastern part of the county. Rebels also arrived in Thetford, spreading revolt in the south-west of the county towards the Fens. The agitators converged on Norwich, Lynn and Swaffham; assembling on Mousehold Heath before marching on Norwich, where they caused considerable damage to the property and possessions of poll tax collectors and officials, destroying legal records such as court rolls and taxation documents as they went. A further attack was made on Great Yarmouth.

Henry Despenser, the 'Warlike Bishop', set off with his own retinue to engage the insurgents and gathered support from those who opposed the rebels as he marched across the county. Litster and his rebels fell back to North Walsham Heath where, on 25 or 26 June 1381, a bloody battle ensued. The rebels were no match for Despenser's better trained and equipped men. The denouement of the battle was the slaughter of the peasants, who had fled to the unconsecrated footings of the new church in North Walsham after they mistakenly believed they might be able to claim sanctuary there. Litster was captured and hanged, drawn and quartered. His remains were displayed in Norwich, Yarmouth, Lynn and his home near North Walsham, as a stern warning to any others who would consider rebellion.

GLADMAN'S RISING, 1443

The Abbot of St Benet at Holme pressed for the removal of the new flour mills that had been built by the city on the Wensum and, in January 1443, it appeared he would have his wish. City folk feared a shortage of flour and, in an attempt to block the abbot's legal process, Robert Toppes (a former mayor) removed the common seal from the Guildhall. A full-scale riot, enflamed by old resentments over the power of the Church, ensued. Rioters, led by such luminaries as the Mayor of Norwich, piled wood against the cathedral gates and threatened to burn the priory down.

In the midst of the commotion, it was arranged for John Gladman (one of the rioters) to ride into the city 'like a crowned king with a sceptre and sword carried before him'. Riding with him were twenty-four others, 'with a crown upon their arms and carrying bows and arrows, as if they were valets of the crown of the lord king', followed by 100 more carrying bows and arrows and swords. They processed around the city and rang the bells to gather the populance to them. It was claimed that they were able to bring together 3,000 people and urged them 'to make a violent insurrection throughout the entire city ... armed with swords, bows and arrows, hauberks and coats of armour'. The rioters held Norwich for a week, but once it was over, accusations were made that their actions were actually a challenge against the king's authority. It was suggested that Gladman's parade had been in mimicry of a royal procession and all those who had followed him were branded as 'rysers ageynst the kyng'.

The consequences of Gladman's Rising were serious for Norwich. The city was fined 3,000 marks (later reduced to 1,000), its liberties were seized by the king and Sir John Clifton of New Buckenham was imposed upon the city to rule it as governor for four years.

KETT'S REBELLION, 1549

On 6 July 1549, the feast of the translation of St Thomas à Becket was celebrated at Wymondham. Recent enclosures of land around the town led locals to rise up and start smashing down fences at Hethersett. When the mob arrived at yeoman Robert Kett's enclosures he sympathised with their cause and joined them in tearing down his own fences.

The rioters mustered again in Wymondham on 8 July and marched on Norwich with Robert Kett at their head. Refused entry to the city, the rebel force made camp upon Mousehold. They established a council headed by Kett, who sat under the 'Oak of Reformation' and drew up a charter of demands righting the wrongs done to commoners. A royal herald came to the camp and offered a pardon but Kett refused, saying they had offended no laws and did not require one, following which a boy stepped forward and defecated in front of the herald to show his contempt. The herald went away denouncing Kett as a traitor. The following day the rebels stormed the city.

A royal army under the Marquess of Northampton arrived at Norwich on 31 July. The rebels initially fell back but then returned again that same night. The fighting, which continued into the early hours, resulted in many deaths, including that of Lord Sheffield. On 23 August, a considerably larger force of 14,000 men arrived at the city led by the Earl of Warwick and another herald offered Kett a pardon but was again rejected. Three days of intense fighting then commenced with the final battle fought upon Dussin's Dale. Some 3,000 rebels were slain, the rebellion was put down and many of the surviving perpetrators were publicly hanged as a warning to others. Kett was captured alive and was paraded through Norwich. At the foot of the castle, a rope was fixed about his neck and he was drawn up to a gibbet upon the battlements and left hanging there until his body wasted away.

THE NORWICH CONSPIRACY, 1570

The great 'Stranger' immigration of 1567 brought a substantial Flemish and Walloon community of Protestant weavers to the City of Norwich to pass on their skills. In the main they seem to have been welcomed, but there were also dissenting voices. George Redman of Cringleford spoke out against the Strangers, claiming they were taking the jobs and livelihood of the citizens of Norwich, and demanding that they should be sent home or he would 'string up the Sheriff' and 'levy a force'. Joined by John Throgmorton, John Appleyard the Sheriff of Norwich and Thomas Brooke of Rollesby, they formed two groups, with Redman raising a force in Cringleford and another being levied at Harleston Fair. Magistrates were informed of these actions and John Throgmorton was first to be apprehended, followed by a number of others. The rising was put down before it really got started and the three ringleaders suffered the dreadful fate of being hanged, drawn and quartered.

THE CIVIL WAR OR THE GREAT BLOWE

On Monday, 24 April 1648, crowds of those loyal to Charles I rose up in Norwich and stormed the headquarters of the county committee, not far from St Peter Mancroft church on what is now known as Bethel Street. When Parliamentarian cavalry arrived to put down the rising, fierce fighting broke out. More arms were looted from the Committee House, but in their haste to break open some gunpowder casks and carry off the contents, rioters spilt a large quantity of it within the building; it ignited and exploded some ninety barrels of gunpowder. To give an idea of the scale of this blast, Guy Fawkes and his conspirators planned to use thirty-six barrels of gunpowder to blow up the Houses of Parliament. What became known as 'The Great Blowe' is believed to have been the largest explosion to take place during the English Civil War. Forty rioters were killed, over 120 were injured and the immediate vicinity was devastated. The explosion blew out the windows of St Peter Mancroft and St Stephen's churches and sent timbers, tiles, wood, plaster, stone, lead debris and bits of victims showering down across the city.

Second Blowe ... Well, Nearly

Another great explosion in the city was only narrowly averted in February 1860 when a fire occurred on the premises of Mr W.C. Aberdein, pastry cook, Dove Street, Norwich. The outbreak itself was not of a serious character but the adjoining premises were owned by Mr Cubitt, an ironmonger, and contained upwards of 400lbs of gunpowder which was safely removed in wet blankets.

NORWICH AND THE NORTH

An artillery company of 100 men was raised in Norwich in 1715 in response to the Rebellion in the North. Another company was raised in the city in 1745 as a consequence of the Jacobite risings in Scotland, with Lord Hobart appointed their commander.

THE CAVALRY BARRACKS

The first purpose-built barracks in Norwich was originally known as the Horse Barracks and was erected by the government on the site of the old Pockthorpe Manor House at a cost of £20,000 in 1791. The buildings were built of brick and formed three sides of a square, the centre being accommodation for officers. The wings accommodated up to 320 men and 266 horses, and the high wall that surrounded the entire barracks and parade ground enclosed an area of 10 acres. On 6 August 1843, a fire, which originated in the forage barn, destroyed the left wing but the men of the Scots Greys succeeded in saving the remainder of the buildings.

Later retitled the Cavalry Barracks, a roll call of many of the mounted units of the British Army quartered there – from hussars and dragoon to lancers and artillery – was published in successive editions of the *Norwich Annual*. In the 1920s, the barracks were initially taken over by the Royal Artillery and given their last change of name to become known as the Nelson Barracks and were used by a number of units during the Second World War, including the Royal Norfolk Regiment. In 1947, the Regular Army handed the old barracks over to the Territorial Army for use as a training centre, however, the building fell into disuse and was finally demolished in 1965 with the majority of the site off Barrack Street being converted into social housing. Today, there is hardly any trace that a barracks ever existed on the site.

List of Regiments Stationed in Norwich Cavalry Barracks.

1793-4	1st (King's) Dragoon Guards
1795	2nd D.G. (Queen's Bays)
1796-7	6th (Inniskilling) Dragoons
1798	4th Dragoons (4th Hussars)
1799	14th Light Dragoons
1800-1	13th L. Dragoons (13th Hus.)
1801	3rd Dragoon Guards
1802	13th Light Dragoons
1803	7th L. Dragoons (7th Hus.)
1804-5	1st (Royal) Dragoons
1806	No Cavalry
1807-8	6th Dragoon Guards
1810-14	No Cavalry
1815	Brunswick Hussars (King's German Legion)
1816	1st (Royal) Dragoons
1817	5th Dragoon Guards
1818	15th (King's) Hussars
1819	9th (Queen's Royal) Lancers
1819-20	14th L. Dragoons (14th Hus.)
1821	4th Light Dragoons
1822	7th Dragoon Guards
1822	1st (Royal) Dragoons
1822	16th (Queen's) Lancers
1823	15th (King's) Hussars
1823	8th (King's R. Irish) Hussars
1824	2nd Dragoon Guards
1825-6	2nd Dragoons (Scots Greys)
1826	1st (King's) Dragoon Guards
1826	Depot 40th Foot
1827	12th Lancers
1828	7th Dragoon Guards
1829	12th Lancers
1830-1	1st (Royal) Dragoons
1832	7th (Queen's Own) Hussars.
1833	3rd L. Dragoons (3rd Hus.)
1834	2nd Dragoon Guards
1835	6th (Inniskilling) Dragoons
1836	17th Lancers
1837	3rd Dragoon Guards
1838	4th Dragoon Guards
1839	9th (Queen's Royal) Lancers
1840	8th Hussars
1841	7th Dragoon Guards
1841-2	13th Light Dragoons
1843	2nd Dragoons (Scots Greys)
1844	4th L. Dragoons (4th Hus.)
1845	7th (Queen's Own) Hussars
1846	6th Dragoon Guards
1847	No Cavalry
1848-9	16th (Queen's) Lancers
1850	11th Hussars
1851	2nd Dragoon Guards
1852	4th L. Dragoons (4th Hus.)

1853	6th Dragoon Guards
1854-5	Royal Artillery
1856	Royal Artillery, 2nd Battery
1857	15th (King's) Hussars
1858-9	Royal Horse Artillery
1860	10th Hussars
1861	5th Dragoon Guards
1862-3	5th (Royal Irish) Lancers
1863	18th Hussars
1864	16th (Queen's) Lancers
1865	13th Hussars
1866	No Cavalry
1867	15th (King's) Hussars
1868-70	Royal Horse Artillery
1871-2	7th Dragoon Guards
1873	3rd Dragoon Guards
1873	Depot 51st and 105th Regts.
1874-5	7th Hussars
1875	6th Dragoon Guards
1876	1st (Royal) Dragoons
1877	5th (Royal Irish) Lancers
1878	21st Hussars
1879	1st (Royal) Dragoons
1879	27th Brigade Depot
1880	6th (Inniskilling) Dragoons
1881	3rd (King's Own) Hussars
1882	7th Dragoon Guards
1883-5	4th Hussars
1885-6	13th Hussars
1886-8	19th Hussars
1888-90	20th Hussars
1891-3	8th Hussars
1894-5	1st Dragoon Guards
1895-8	7th Dragoon Guards
1898-9	7th Hussars
1900-1	13th Hussars
1901	No Cavalry
1902	Army Service Corps
1902-3	3rd Dragoon Guards
1903	Four Provisional Regiments
1904	Prov. Regiment of Cavalry
1905	2nd Dragoons (Scots Greys)
1906-8	7th Hussars
1909	19th Hussars
1910-12	16th Lancers
1912-14	12th Lancers
1915-19	No Cavalry
1919	7th Dragoon Guards
1919-23	Royal Field Artillery
1923-24	78th and 85th Batt., R.F.A.
1924-25	15th, 20th, 21st Pack Batts., Royal Field Artillery
1928	4th Light Brigade, R.A.
1928-36	3rd Light Brigade, R.A.

FLANDERS IN FLANNEL

In December 1793, subscriptions were made in the city to supply our soldiers serving in Flanders with flannel waistcoats.

THE GENERAL

One of the most outstanding military figures of Norwich in the late eighteenth and early nineteenth centuries was Lieutenant General John Money CB (Companion of the Order of Bath), KC, who was also colonel of the 2nd Regiment of Dragoons and 3rd Regiment of Norfolk Volunteer Yeomanry Cavalry.

Money entered the army in 1794, serving as a volunteer in Elliott's Light Horse during the Seven Years' War and was with them at the Battle of Tillinghaussen. He was afterwards a captain in the 9th (East Norfolk) Regiment of Foot during the American War of Independence and served as deputy assistant quartermaster general under General Burgoyne.

Major Money was also a daring balloonist. In 1785, he ascended in a balloon from Quantrell's Gardens in the city but was driven 7 leagues from land. The balloon crashed into the sea and the *Argus* revenue cutter picked up Money – who was lucky to escape with his life – around five hours later, 18 miles from Southwold.

In 1800, Money took part in the expedition to Cadiz. He also served in Egypt in 1801, the Peninsula Campaigns of 1811 and 1812 (where he was present at the Siege of Badajoz and the Battle of Salamanca) and was at Quatre Bras and on the field of Waterloo in 1815. He was promoted to general and was one of the oldest officers in the British service. Money published a number of useful pamphlets on military and other subjects and was the man who built Crown Point. He died aged 77 at Crown Point, Trowse on 25 August 1858.

ONE OF THE OLD BRIGADE

Thomas Harrison was born in the city in 1795 and saw much active service as a soldier. He joined the 69th Regiment at the age of 17, was taken prisoner at the bombardment of Antwerp, was present at Waterloo, went out to India (where he was under arms for fourteen years), took part in the first expedition to Burma and, on returning to England in 1832, was rewarded with a pension of 15*d* per day. He died on 29 March 1886 and was buried at the Rosary cemetery.

SWORD WITH A STORY

The sword that the Spanish admiral, Don Xavier Francisco Winthuysen, surrendered to Lord Nelson while dying of his wounds at the Battle of St Vincent on 14 February 1797, was presented to the City of Norwich by the great admiral and placed in a mural monument at the Guildhall.

SOME NORWICH VOLUNTEER FORCES

The Norwich Light Horse Volunteers were formed in February 1797. John Harvey, captain of this force, is remembered in a painting by Mr Opie, which was placed in St Andrew's Hall at the request of the troop in 1803.

The following list of parochial corps of volunteers and their respective commanders were all raised in Norwich in 1798:

Mancroft Volunteers – Captain John Browne
St Stephen's – Captain Hardy
East Norwich – Captain Thomas Blake Junior
St Peter's Parmountergate – Captain Herring
St Saviour's and St Clement's – Captain Fisk
St Andrew's – Captain J.A. Murray

The Norwich Regiment of Volunteer Infantry was raised with 800 men in August 1803 under Lieutenant Colonel John Patteson.

On 18 January 1804, the Norwich Regiment took the Oath of Allegiance. They received their colours in an impressive ceremony, presided over by the mayor and attended by the court of aldermen, which was held in the Market Place.

The Norwich Juvenile Regiment of Infantry, a cadet corps armed with dummy muskets and tin bayonets, were presented with colours by 'a young lady of the city' in January 1804.

Norwich was appointed a garrison town by the government, the different volunteer regiments were brigaded, and did permanent duty at Yarmouth, Norwich and Lynn.

The Norwich Volunteers were disbanded after the establishment of the local militia in 1813.

The last surviving member of the Norwich Regiment of Volunteers was its paymaster-sergeant, Stephen Wilde. He had been governor of the city gaol for many years and died on Unthank Road, in his 96th year, in January 1878.

ANGLO-DUTCH CONFLICT

After the defeat of the Dutch fleet by Admiral Duncan on 11 October 1797, the British ships returned to Yarmouth and many British sailors were brought to the Norfolk and Norwich Hospital for treatment. A dinner was held in their honour at Keymer's Gardens.

THE BRAVE SAILOR BOY

In July 1798, a 13-year-old sailor named Roberts clambered up to and got out of the highest window of the cathedral spire. He then – assisted only by the crockets, which are above 1yd apart – climbed to the finial that crowns the summit of the spire. On this narrow footing, at a height of above 300ft, he walked twice round the spire and then, in the presence of a vast crowd who had assembled to watch the feat, he amused himself twirling round the weathercock with the utmost composure, before safely returning to the window again to the amazement of beholders.

THE THREAT OF INVASION

In late summer 1803, active preparations commenced for the defence of the county in view of a possible invasion. On 8 August, several officers and non-commissioned officers of the 47th Regiment of Foot arrived in Norwich to receive the balloted men and substitutes of the Army of Reserve, the training of whom commenced the next day in Chapel Field. A county meeting was held at the Shirehall on the 10th and resolutions were passed, assuring King George III of the readiness of the county to take defensive measures. On the 16th, a meeting of the inhabitants of Norwich was held at the Guildhall and a subscription was opened for raising a regiment of volunteer infantry. Clerks enrolled the names of the volunteers, and the city flag was displayed from the window of the town clerk's office. By the following day, 702 men had pledged themselves, and by Saturday the 20th, the number had increased to 1,085. The public subsciption was receieved with similar success and exceeded £3,000, of which £500 was given by the Corporation.

On 26 August, the regiment was formed, 800 strong, under Lieutenant Colonel Harvey (commanding), Lieutenant Colonel Plumptre, and Major Sigismund Trafford. The public subscription then amounted to £6,400. A rifle corps was also formed, with Mr R.M. Bacon as captain, and at Yarmouth, 500 persons enrolled under the command of Lieutenant Colonel William Gould. On the 27th, it was announced that the number of volunteers in the county (about 7,300) enabled the Lord Lieutenant to suspend the compulsory clauses of the Defence Act. The government purchased some properties in Norwich to be converted into temporary barracks for the reception of the 800 infantry.

WE SAW THE SIGNAL

During the invasion scare of 1803, telegraphs, signal flags, or tar barrels were stationed on all the churches and lofty edifices along the coast, providing a chain of communication to pass intelligence, either by night or day, of the event of the enemy's landing. In 1804, flagstaffs were placed at Raynham Hall, Holkham Hall and Houghton Hall. The red flag was only to be hoisted in the event of an actual invasion or on the appearance of an enemy on the coast. A more permanent telegraph was erected upon the hill at Thorpe in December 1807, and the following year the chain of telegraphs ran from Strumpshaw, Thorpe Hills, Honingham, Carlton, Harling and from thence between Thetford and Bury, over Newmarket Heath to London. This meant that telegraph orders from the London Admiralty office to Yarmouth, and vice versa, could be achieved in seventeen minutes.

YOUNGEST OFFICER AT TRAFALGAR

Frederic Lea White, third son of William White of Norwich, entered the Royal Navy as a first-class volunteer on 3 September 1805 when he was not quite 13 (having been born on 9 September 1792). He was aboard HMS *Africa* at Trafalgar and was deep in the fight. White had his thigh fractured and was rated midshipman for his gallant conduct in his first fight. Despite never fully recovering from his injury, he saw plenty of action between 1805 and 1812, including the evacuation of troops from Corunna. Gazetted lieutenant in 1812, White only received commander's rank when he left the navy in 1843. He died in 1859 and was buried in Norwich.

NELSON'S RIGHT ARM

Sir Edward Berry, flag captain to Lord Nelson at the Battle of the Nile, lived at The Warren in Old Catton between 1814 and 1822. A story told about Berry relates to when he was at court with Nelson and the king; a remark was made about the loss of Nelson's right arm but the great admiral simply pointed to Berry and said, 'This is my right arm'.

NELSON'S STATUE

Thomas Milnes' Portland stone statue of Admiral Lord Nelson was originally erected in front of the Guildhall in 1852; however, on 16 April 1856 it was removed to a new site in the Upper Close on the suggestion of Sir Richard Westmacott, Professor of Sculpture. It is still in evidence immediately facing the Norwich School where Nelson was briefly a pupil. The first celebration of the anniversary of Trafalgar was observed in Norwich on the initiation of the Navy League on 21 October 1896 with the decoration of the Nelson statue.

WATERLOO HERO

Norwich-born Robert Forster, formerly bandmaster of the 33rd (Duke of Wellington's Own) Regiment, served at Waterloo where he was shot in the knee. Forster was the only survivor of the band, the whole having fallen by his side at Waterloo. The pistol ball was never extracted from Forster's knee. He died aged 70, at Bethel Street, Norwich, on 21 May 1854.

THE LAST NORWICH CHARGER

The last Norwich born survivor of the Charge of the Light Brigade at the Battle of Balaclava on 25 October 1854 was Mr George Wilde, who died aged 62 at his home on Gladstone Street on 18 May 1887. He had been a trooper in the 13th Light Dragoons, during the charge his horse was killed and he was wounded.

WELLINGTON'S STATUE

The statue of the Duke of Wellington, victor of Waterloo, was originally erected in Norwich Market Place opposite Davy Place and was unveiled by Mayor Sir Samuel Bignold on 2 November 1854 in the presence of 20,000 spectators. The statue cost about £1,000 and Wellington is represented in the identical boots, cloak and some other portions of dress that were actually worn by him at Waterloo; the articles themselves were placed at the disposal of Mr G.G. Adams, the sculptor, when he was modelling the figure. The statue was moved to the cathedral close in 1937.

A HERO'S RETURN

General Sir Charles Ashe Windham was welcomed back to his native county on 1 August 1856 with great celebration. The hero of the Battle of the Great Redan, a key engagement during the Crimean War, was presented with congratulatory addresses at various stations along the route to Norwich. A banquet, attended by officers of the army and navy connected with Norfolk and Norwich who had served in the Crimea, was given in his honour at St Andrew's Hall.

RIFLE VOLUNTEERS

On 23 May 1859, a meeting of citizens was held in the Guildhall, Norwich and it was resolved to raise a Norwich Rifle Corps. Their uniform was to consist of a long grey tunic with black mohair braid, buttons down the centre and a low upright collar; trousers were to be of the same colour, with a headdress of plumed grey shako of hair cloth and an equipment belt and pouch bag of black leather. All volunteers would buy their uniform at a cost 'not exceeding £4'. By 5 July, the first three companies had been formed and their headquarters were established in the old Militia Barracks at St Catherine's Close. The Norwich Rifle Volunteers, under the command of Lieutenant Colonel Boileau, proceeded by special train to Windsor and took part in the volunteer review before the queen in the Great Park on 9 July 1881.

THE DRILL HALL, CHAPEL FIELD

The foundation stone of the first purpose-built volunteer drill hall in the city was laid by Mrs Nichols, the mayoress, on 24 May 1866. It was the day of the queen's birthday and a parade of the 1st Norfolk Light Horse Volunteers and the Artillery and Rifle Volunteers had been held in Chapel Field after the stone-laying ceremony luncheon was served at St Andrew's Hall. Built to the designs of the city surveyor, James Benest, it was opened with due ceremony by the Prince of Wales on 30 October 1866.

It was to the officer's mess here that King Edward VII retired for luncheon during his official visit on 25 October 1909. Volunteer battalions of the Norfolk Regiment had mustering there for the South African War in 1900 and the hall would become the headquarters for Territorials of the 4th Battalion who mobilised for the two world wars there. Sadly, by the 1960s it was seen as outdated by the army and, with the Grapes Hill and Chapel Field inner link road development scheme looming, the drill hall was demolished in 1963.

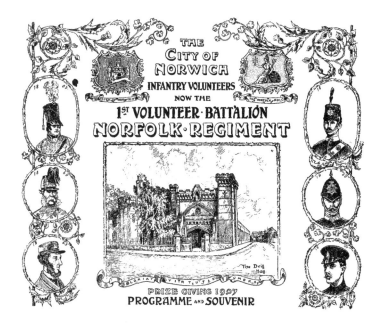

THE SOLDIERS' MEMORIAL

Lord Waveney unveiled a monument in Norwich cemetery on 17 October 1878, to commemorate 'the memory of deceased soldiers of regiments stationed in this city or who may die while on service here'. Designed by Mr John Bell, a Norfolk man, the monument was called *The Spirit of the Army* and a figure formed the finial, cast in terracotta by Messrs Doulton of the Lambeth Pottery.

BRITANNIA BARRACKS

Back in 1883, Dr Peter Eade, the then Mayor of Norwich, arranged the purchase of a 10-acre site to the north of Plumstead Road for the building of a barracks. The War Office had informed the city that, if it could provide the land, the depot of the Norfolk Regiment would be established there. So keen were the citizens of Norwich to see a barracks built that they raised £1,600 by public subscription, making it possible for the Corporation to buy the site (costing £1,000) from the church commissioners.

The balance of the money was spent on purchasing the land and the creation of an access road, which became known as Barrack Road off Plumstead Road. The main blocks of Britannia Barracks were built in 1886–87 by Norwich City Council and presented to the Norfolk Regiment as its first permanent depot. Serving the soldiers of the regiment through two world wars, the Royal Norfolk Regiment was amalgamated with the Suffolk Regiment on 24 August 1959 to become 1st Battalion, East Anglian Regiment and, on moving to a new location in Bury St Edmunds, Britannia Barracks ceased to be the depot of the county regiment and the buildings were handed over to units of the Territorial Army in September 1959. The Territorial Army moved out in 1967 and Norwich Prison took over the barracks site, with the exception of Cameron House, which continued to serve as the Royal Norfolk Regiment Museum, Royal Anglian Regiment HQ, Regimental Association and services administration offices. In 1990, the Regimental Museum was removed to the Shirehall, the offices moved elsewhere soon after and Britannia Barracks lost its final links with the military.

A CHARGER

Thomas Frederick Armes, bugle major of the 1st Volunteer Battalion Norfolk Regiment, was formerly in the 4th Light Dragoons and took part in the famous Charge of the Light Brigade at the Battle of Balaclava, in which he was wounded and left for dead on the field. He died at his home in All Saints Green in January 1885.

SIR GARNET WOLSELEY

On 19 December 1895, Field Marshal Sir Garnet Joseph Wolseley, commander-in-chief of the British Army, visited Norwich for the purpose of inaugurating the Soldiers' and Sailors' Home in Queen Street. The Sir Garnet pub in the Market Place was named after the well-loved field marshal in 1874.

THE ROYAL NORFOLK VETERAN'S ASSOCIATION

Years before the creation of the British Legion, one of the very first veterans' associations in the country was begun in Norwich. The Norfolk Veteran's Association, formally founded by Captain

A.M. Atthill in 1898, had a charter to 'rescue from the workhouse or pauper's grave any old soldier, sailor or marine who through no fault of his own is reduced to destitution'. Their good work was recognised by Edward VII when he conferred the title 'Royal' upon the association and even presented them colours to be carried when they were on parade.

THE HAPPY PADRE

The Revd Samuel F. Leighton Green MC (Military Cross) and Bar (author of *The Happy Padre*, an account of his experiences as a military chaplain on the Western Front) was appointed curate of St Bartholomew's church, Heigham in 1904 and ordained the following year. In 1912, he moved to St Barnabas, the other church in the parish, and did much to help those who suffered in the floods that occurred in the city that same year.

After his service in the First World War, Leighton Green was appointed honorary chaplain to the forces and returned to St Barnabas. In 1921, he was appointed rector of All Saints church, Mundesley, where he died as incumbent and was buried with full military honours in the churchyard in 1929.

A WARNING ON HORSEBACK

Mounted troops were sent as a display of military force in times of riot or industrial unrest as late as the twentieth century. The last such instances involving mounted troops from Norwich, occurred when a squadron of the 16th Lancers were sent to Salford (with other units) during the Manchester and Salford dockers and carters strike in July 1911 and during the colliery riots in Lancashire in April 1912.

MARATHON RIDE OF CADET DESPATCH RIDERS

Colour Sergeant Vickers and Bombardier Strett of the Cadet Norfolk Artillery, both just 15 years of age, carried a despatch from Captain R.C.O. Crosskill, their commanding officer, to the Mansion House in London – a distance of 112 miles. Designed to be part of a training exercise, their journey began at 3.10 p.m. on the afternoon of Thursday, 30 October 1913 and they arrived in London the following day at 6 p.m., despite bad roads and inclement weather. The Lord Mayor entrusted them with return messages, which they undertook to convey to their commandant. Their achievement was even reported in *The Times*.

THE FIRST WORLD WAR

Enemy Agents

During the First World War there were a number of spy scares across the country but they were particularly acute in Norfolk. On 10 August 1914, German waiters, arrested by troops at Cromer under the Defence of the Realm Act, were displayed in Norwich Market Place as German spies.

Proud Mother

Mrs Mary Ann Clabburn of Norwich had seven sons serving in the Norfolk Regiment in September 1914.

Comforts for the Troops

Mrs Grissell, wife of Captain Bernard Grissell of the Norfolk Regiment, ran a comforts scheme from their home at The Grange on Thorpe Road for the men of the regiment out on active service in France and Flanders in 1914. As part of this service she requested a range of items for sending out to those at the front, including handkerchiefs of inconspicuous colouring, bootlaces, illustrated papers and magazines, chocolate, peppermints, acid tablets and drops, lime juice jujubes, cigarettes, tobacco pouches and boracic powder, indelible pencils, playing cards, dominoes, pocketknives and fancy soap. Shirts were to be made of dark grey or khaki flannel, with tin buttons firmly sewn on and cotton collar bands measuring 15.5in or 16.5in. The feet of any socks donated were stipulated to be 10.5in long.

The First ANZAC Casualty at Gallipoli

Lance Corporal Arthur Joshua Martins and 'Banjo' Reeves of 14 Platoon, D Company, 12th Battalion Australian Imperial Force, were struck by Turkish bullets while still on the deck of HMS *Chelmer*, shortly before alighting into the whaler to row ashore at ANZAC Cove around 4 a.m. on 25 April 1915. Sadly, the wounds that Lance Corporal Martins received to his chest proved fatal and he was the first mortally wounded soldier of what became known as 'ANZAC Day'. He was not, however, an Australian by birth, but actually a Norwich man who had emigrated to Australia a few years before the outbreak of war. His mother, Mrs A.J. Martins of No. 4 Terrace Lane, Lakenham, was left mourning the loss of her 26-year-old son.

A Tragic Tale of a Brave Soldier

Private Albert Sepple of the Leicestershire Regiment was evacuated back to Blighty and admitted to the Norfolk War Hospital in Thorpe after being badly wounded at the Battle of Ypres on 6 June 1915. He had twelve fragments of shrapnel in his brain and lived for twenty weeks without losing consciousness except when under anaesthetics. Surgeons managed to remove the twelve pieces, which ranged in size from a pinhead to a large pea. In addition to his head injuries, Private Sepple's right side was paralysed, he had suffered a large wound to his left shoulder and his left knee was shattered. Nevertheless, his courage never wavered and he was often heard to whistle while in his hospital bed. Sadly his strength left him and he finally passed away on 21 October 1915. His body was returned to his hometown of Guildford for burial.

The First Women's Fire Brigade

A large number of Chamberlin's Fire Brigade members joined the army and in September 1915, Chamberlin's Ltd in Norwich established a ladies' brigade, the first of its kind in the Eastern Counties. The main objective was to establish an efficient body of firefighters who could deal with an outbreak of fire following a Zeppelin bombing raid. The captain and sub-captain were men but all the other members were female members of the firm.

The Greatest Heroine of the First World War

Edith Cavell is generally hailed as the greatest British heroine of the First World War. While working as the matron of L'École Belge d' Infirmières Diplômées in Brussels, she was arrested by the German invaders and tried for 'conducting soldiers to the enemy'. Found guilty, she was shot by a German firing squad at the Tir Nationale (National Rifle Range) on 12 October 1915.

Born on 4 December 1865, the daughter of the Rector of Swardeston, Cavell returned to Norwich several times during her training years. She often attended Holy Trinity church when she was staying with her widowed mother in Norwich, and it was in this church that the first mark of remembrance and acknowledgement of Nurse Cavell's sacrifice was made, in the form of a reredos unveiled by the bishop on Sunday, 10 September 1916. The inscription bore her last words: 'Patriotism is not enough. I must have no hatred or bitterness towards anyone.'

The Tombland memorial to Nurse Cavell was originally erected in front of the Maid's Head Hotel and was unveiled by Queen Alexandra on 12 October 1918. The nurses' home that stood next to the hotel was also dedicated to Nurse Cavell and was opened by the queen on the same day. After the war, Nurse Cavell's body was exhumed and returned for burial at Life's Green, at the east side of Norwich Cathedral, on 15 May 1919.

Bravest of the Brave

Norfolk's most highly decorated soldier of the First World War was Sergeant Harry Cator VC (Victoria Cross), MM (Military Medal), CdeG (Croix de Guerre). Harry was born on 24 January 1884, the son of a railway worker at Drayton. He got married on 2 September 1914, enlisted the following day and proceeded to France with 7th Battalion, East Surrey Regiment on 23 June 1915. He received his first award, the Military Medal for bravery in the field, for his conduct during the Battle of the Somme in 1916 and he was also decorated with France's Croix de Guerre avec Palme for helping to rescue thirty-six men who had become tangled in enemy barbed wire in no-man's-land.

Harry's Victoria Cross was awarded for action at Hangest Trench during the Battle of Arras on 19 April 1917. His citation states:

> For most conspicuous bravery and devotion to duty. Whilst consolidating the first line captured system his platoon suffered severe casualties from hostile machine-gun and rifle fire. In full view of the enemy and under heavy fire Sergeant Cator, with one man, advanced to attack the hostile machine gun. The man accompanying him was killed after going a short distance, but Sergeant Cator continued on and picking up a Lewis gun and some drums on his way succeeded in reaching the northern end of the hostile trench. Meanwhile, one of our bombing parties was seen to be held up by a machine gun. Sergeant Cator took up a position from which he sighted this gun and killed the entire team and the officer whose papers he brought in.

He continued to hold that end of the trench with the Lewis gun and with such effect that the bombing squad was enabled to work along, the result being that one hundred prisoners and five machine guns were captured.

Three days later he was severely wounded by a bursting shell that shattered his jaw. He recovered from his wounds and was presented with his VC by HM King George V at Buckingham Palace on 21 July 1917. Harry passed away on 7 April 1966 and is buried in Sprowston cemetery, near Norwich.

Norwich Boy is a Suffolk Regiment Hero

Sidney James Day was born on St Anne's Lane off King Street, Norwich on 3 July 1891. Educated at St Mark's School, Lakenham, he was a choirboy at the church and a sergeant in the Church Lad's Brigade. On 26 August 1917, Day was a corporal serving in the 11th Battalion, Suffolk Regiment at Priel Wood, Malakoff Farm (east of Hargicourt in France), in command of a bombing section clearing a maze of enemy trenches. This he did, killing two machine gunners and taking four prisoners. On reaching a point where the trench had been levelled, he went on alone and made his way along to the left in order to win through to the neighbouring troops. Immediately on his return to his section, a stick bomb fell into the trench occupied by two officers (one badly wounded) and three other ranks. Corporal Day seized the bomb and threw it over the trench, where it instantly exploded. This prompt action saved the lives of those in the trench. He afterwards completed the clearing of the trench and established himself in an advanced position, remaining for sixty-six hours at his post even under intense hostile shell, grenade, and rifle fire.

Holyboy Hero

One of the most highly decorated men of the Norfolk Regiment in the First World War was Norwich man Sergeant Bertie James Guymer of 9th (Service) Battalion. Awarded the Military Medal in July 1917, he was presented with the Bar for another brave action in June 1918. His highest award came from an action on 9 October 1918, near Bohain on the border of France and Belgium. Sergeant Guymer was in charge of a platoon and led his men forward through a thick fog with great courage and ability. In spite of heavy machine-gun enfilade fire he pushed on to his objective, surprising sixteen of the enemy in a dugout, whom he captured. In a further action on 11 October, near Vaux-Andigny, he led his platoon forward again under heavy machine-gun fire; his company commander recorded that his 'conduct throughout was excellent' and Guymer received the Distinguished Conduct Medal.

The Lone American

The only American soldier to die in Norwich during the First World War was Sergeant Arthur F. Taylor (26) of Los Angeles, California, who tragically died after his pleasure boat capsized on the River Wensum in the city in July 1918.

We Made It!

During the First World War, Norwich businesses were not found slacking! Howlett & White Ltd, just one of a number of large-scale boot and shoe-making businesses in Norwich, made 453,000 pairs of boots and shoes for the British Army, 32,000 for the Allies and 21,000 British Aviation Boots during the First World War. The Norwich-based engineering firm Boulton & Paul Ltd went into aircraft production and made 2,530 aircraft (notably F.E. 2Bs, Sopwith Camels and Snipes) and 7,835 propellers in their Norwich factories. Norwich Components Ltd made thousands of fuses, Laurence & Scott made shells for 60-pounder guns and Barnards Ltd Engineers produced over 6,994 miles of wire netting for the War Office and Admiralty.

Boys of the Old Brigade

During the First World War and in the years that followed, a number of ex-servicemen's association branches were created in the city, including the Old Contemptibles, the Comrades of the Great War, the Better 'Ole Club and, of course, the British Legion. In April 1963, the Lord Mayor, Mr L. Howes, launched an appeal for £500 to enable thirty-four First World War Norfolk veterans to revisit the Ypres battlefield. One can only imagine the memories they shared.

FOREWARNED IS FOREARMED

In October 1933 the Air Defence Intelligence System was extended to include the counties of Dorset, Norfolk and Suffolk. The inaugural meeting for the formation and recruitment for the Observer Corps (OC) in Norfolk was held at the Norwich Lad's Club in early 1934, but the planned recruitment talk was found to be unnecessary because Mr John Dain, the chief constable of Norwich, had already spoken to a number of likely local contacts and had mustered all the volunteers initially required for the new OC unit from the offices of Norwich Union. By the end of November 1934 there were thirty-four OC posts across the county and a centre of operations room in a semi-basement under the Norwich Telephone Exchange at the corner of Dove Street and Guildhall Hill. The area to be known as 16 Group (Southern Area) was ready and became operational on 1 March 1935 with S.C. 'Nobby' Spalding as the first group controller.

THE SECOND WORLD WAR

The Winds of War
The first batch of 300 Anderson shelters reached Norwich in late August 1939. These shelters were freely supplied to all homes with an income that did not exceed £250 a year and with a suitable garden. Made from pre-formed corrugated sheet-steel, the Anderson was supplied in twenty-one pieces with a bag of nuts and bolts. The householder (and helpful neighbours) would dig out the ground, assemble the shelter and pile earth back on top. In Norwich there were also the trench shelters supplemented by sixty surface shelters. Quicker and easier to build than the underground type, these public shelters could hold up to fifty people and were constructed with 14in brickwork which claimed to be blast and splinter proof. The first of these shelters were constructed around the Cattle Market and on terraced streets where there were concreted and paved backyards rather than gardens.

Evacuees
The first party of about 1,000 evacuated children arrived in Norwich on the morning of 1 September 1939 and were found homes by the same afternoon. However, as the day wore on, it became more difficult to find places for subsequent arrivals, particularly when more children came into Norwich than were expected. Some children ended up spending an uncomfortable night sleeping in church halls, but great efforts were made by local people and the adults that accompanied the children to make the best of the situation.

Room for More!
Shortly after war was declared in September 1939, the large number of volunteers wishing to join up swamped the recruiting offices and, as a result, a combined navy, army and RAF recruiting centre was opened at the Norwich Agricultural Hall.

First Norwich Prisoner of War in the Second World War

The first Norwich serviceman to be confirmed and reported in the national press as a prisoner of war was Petty Officer A. Webster, who was taken prisoner – along with the rest of the crew – when the submarine HMS *Starfish* was sunk by a depth charge from a German minesweeper at Heligoland Bight on 9 January 1940.

On the Land

A meeting of the Norfolk Agricultural Wages Committee was held at Norwich in February 1940. It agreed to raise the wages by 1*s* 6*d* a week to 38*s* for Norfolk agricultural labourers, and by 2*s* 6*d* for all special class workers: to 45*s* 6*d* for cowmen and 44*s* 6*d* for horsemen and shepherds.

Dad's Army

Lieutenant Colonel Bassett F. Hornor DSO was commissioned to raise a City of Norwich unit of Local Defence Volunteers and, on 17 May 1940, the 10th Battalion was established. Within three days, 500 men fell in at the Chapel Field Drill Hall and twenty-four hours later, nightly guards and patrols were on duty throughout the garrison area.

The shortage of weapons became so acute as the number of volunteers increased that old muskets dating back to the Crimean War were borrowed from Norwich Castle Museum for training purposes. A signal company under Captain E.H. Coe MC was rapidly formed and Lieutenant P. Smyth established a tank-hunting platoon. A number of women also supported the battalion as auxiliaries, acting as drivers, signallers and nurses.

In 1941 the battalion formed a guard of honour for the visit of the Chancellor of the Exchequer to Norwich. In 1942, detachments paraded for inspection by the late Duke of Kent and in 1944 they paraded for King George VI. Captain Miller commanded the Norfolk Home Guard contingent, which took part in the final parade in London on Stand Down. During the battalion's active life, two men lost their lives when on duty and a number were wounded. At its demobilisation in November 1944, the strength of the unit was 113 officers and 2,495 other ranks.

Air Raid!

Norwich suffered its first air raid on 9 July 1940, which saw bombs fall on Barnard's Ltd on Salhouse Road, injuring a few people. A number of female employees from Carrow Works were killed when a bomb fell near Carrow Hill as they were walking home from work. Male and female employees were killed with direct hits on Boulton & Paul's Riverside Works and more casualties were caused after four bombs dropped on Thorpe Station sheds and goods yard. Some of those taken to hospital died later from the injuries they had sustained during the raid.

During the Second World War, a total 340 people died during the air raids on Norwich and many more were injured. Over 30,000 houses were damaged, 2,000 of them beyond repair.

The Best of British

An often forgotten fact from the Second World War is that restaurants were exempt from rationing, which led to a certain amount of resentment as the more affluent could supplement their food allowance by eating out. To restrict this, certain rules were put into force: no meal could cost more than 5*s*, no meal could consist of more than three courses, and meat and fish could not be served at the same sitting.

For those who had not managed their coupons, so-called 'Community Feeding Centres' (later renamed British Restaurants) were set up across the country by the Ministry of Food. British Restaurants also came with their own restrictions. No customer could be served a meal that included more than one portion of meat, fish, game, poultry, eggs, or cheese purchased for more than 9*d*. The standard of food was very dependent on the skill of the cooks and what foodstuff was available. The first British Restaurant in Norwich was opened by the Lord Mayor at Bull Close School on 14 July 1940.

Trailer Pumps

By 1940 there were approximately 100 Coventry Victor trailer pumps stationed in the Norwich area with approximately 100 full-time auxiliary firemen and 200 part-time auxiliary firemen to man them.

MAGNA Magic

A unique organisation was established in Norwich between July 1940 and August 1941. The Mutual Aid Good Neighbours Association (MAGNA) was raised with the intention of co-operating with the Air Raid Precautions (ARP) and other allied organisations to provide aid and assistance for the victims of air raids, particularly those who were suffering from shock, and to alleviate the distress of those rendered homeless after an attack. Staffed along the lines of the ARP, an appeal was launched for over 2,000 volunteers to find a 'Street Mother' for every street. The organiser for the city was the indefatigable Mrs Ruth Hardy. She saw MAGNA grow to a membership of over 30,000 Norwich women, who offered their homes as shelter and temporary accommodation to their neighbours. Every one of them displayed a small yellow poster in their window stating 'A good neighbour lives here'.

One for the Ladies

Women who served in uniformed organisations such as the Woman's Land Army were, nonetheless, not considered to be 'in the services' and were not permitted to use forces canteens. Accordingly, a club for 'Women in the Services, the Land Army and Nursing Services' was formally opened on Elm Hill by Mrs Colman on 13 September 1940. Excellent meals could be obtained here; there was also an information bureau, supplies of chocolate and cigarettes to buy, and a lounge with a radio, newspapers and magazines. For 1s, members could even take a bath. The club superintendent was Molly Kent, a former Land Girl who was always especially pleased to welcome members of her 'old mob'.

Danger UXB

On 24 September 1940, the men of 8 Section, 4 Bomb Disposal Company, Royal Engineers, went to work on a 250kg bomb which had smashed through the path and embedded itself 30ft down into the soft subsoil outside No. 4 Theatre Street Norwich. It took a total of four days to uncover and defuse the bomb; it was no easy task and one that could easily have resulted in death and destruction.

By remarkable coincidence, 24 September 1940 was also the day that the George Medal was introduced in recognition of acts of bravery. December 1940 saw an unparalleled award ceremony to reward three members of 8 Section for their role in the successful disposal of the bomb.

Firefighters in Norwich

After London had suffered the Blitz, a scheme was developed between Norwich and the capital which saw twenty London firemen come to the city for a week's holiday in November 1940 while a similar number of firemen from the Norwich force went down to take their place. Rather than take a holiday, however, the London firemen all volunteered to serve with the city fire brigade until the Norwich lads returned.

Yeomanry Hero

The most highly decorated soldier of the Norfolk Yeomanry and one of the most decorated Norwich men in the Second World War was Sergeant Everett John 'Dolly' Gray DCM (Distinguished Conduct Medal), MM of 258 Battery, 65th (Norfolk Yeomanry) Anti-Tank Regiment. Both of his awards were for actions in the Western Desert. He gained his Military Medal for bravery in the field on 13 December 1941 when, during an attack to the west of Gabr el Abidi, he commanded his gun with coolness and courage under exceptionally heavy shell and small-arms fire. During the action, his gun received two direct hits and was temporarily put out of action. Most of his men were killed or wounded and, despite being wounded in two places himself, Gray still successfully made sure his gun was unusable by enemy forces.

Gray was awarded his Distinguished Conduct Medal for action on 25 October 1942. This was the second morning of the Battle of El Alamein, at the 'January' bridgehead and, at first light, the enemy was seen to be grouping for an attack. The troop commander set off to contact the tank commander and ordered Gray to liaise with an infantry post on the flank of the troop. The post turned out to be one which had been reoccupied by the enemy but Gray, quite undaunted and facing fire at close range, brought back six fully armed Italian officers and later some 200 Italian other ranks with the help of only one of his own men. Gray was wounded when the party conducting the prisoners was shelled and he had to be evacuated but was able to return to his unit. The post was found to contain a veritable armoury of heavy machine guns, anti-tank guns, mortars, rifles and light machine guns. By his fearless example and aggressive spirit, with which he imbued his whole troop, Gray was to a large degree responsible both for saving his troop from a very difficult situation and for capturing 200 prisoners. 'Dolly' Gray remains an affectionately remembered character of the Norfolk Yeomanry.

The Weird in Wartime

One of the strangest books published during the Second World War was entitled *Back from the Beyond together with some Spirit Messages on the War*. Compiled by Henry R. Muskett, through the mediumship of Alice S. Muskett, it was published by Roberts Printers, Ten Bell Lane, Norwich in 1942 and cost only 2s 6d. Muskett was known to hold séances and grieving mothers and family members went to him in order to communicate with their lost relations.

Monocles in the Navy

Chief Petty Officer Electrical Artificer Philip Morter of Swardeston was an instrument maker before the outbreak of war and had worn a monocle for a number of years before he volunteered for the

Royal Navy. A rating with a monocle was so much of a naval precedent a ruling had to be laid down and soon there appeared in Admiralty Fleet Orders: 'Monocular Vision – subject to non-interference with the efficient discharge of his duties a naval rating may make a choice between spectacles and a monocle in favour of the latter.'

The Baedeker Blitz

After the failure of the bombing campaigns to destroy airfields and London, Hitler planned to break British morale by destroying the picturesque and historic cities of England.

The cities were reputedly selected from the German Baedeker tourist guide to Britain and the first attack was launched against Exeter on 23 April 1942, a direct reprisal raid for the bombing of Lübeck. German propagandist Baron Gustav Braun von Sturm is reported to have said after the first attack of the campaign, 'We shall go out and bomb every building in Britain marked with three stars in the Baedeker Guide', and thus the so-called 'Three Star Blitz' or 'Baedeker blitz' became the name given by the British to these infamous raids on Exeter, Bath, Norwich, York and Canterbury in April–June 1942. On the nights of 27/28 and 29/30 April 1942, Norwich received its heaviest raids of the war.

AIR RAID SHELTER

HELEN McKIE

Time for a Cuppa

The twenty Church Army canteen vans in Norwich served 10,000 cups of tea during the air raids of April 1942.

Here Come the Americans

American servicemen often took some of their leave in Norwich: dancing at the Samson and Hercules; taking in a movie at cinemas like the Odeon on Botolph Street or Haymarket, and the Regent and Electric on Prince of Wales Road; or perhaps seeing a show at the Hippodrome Theatre or Theatre Royal, or at the YMCA on St Giles where free concerts were given on Sunday evenings. Many just enjoyed a day strolling around the historic sites of the city and the parks at Eaton and Earlham. The American Red Cross Service Club was set up in the Bishop's Palace and US servicemen were provided with dormitories for their visits in the city at No. 13 The Close and at an annex on Bethel Street. It was often the case that thousands of men and women passed through the club in a single month, with around 1,000 staying in the city overnight.

On 24 November 1944, USAAF B-24 Liberator *Lady Jane* from 753rd Squadron, 458th Bomb Group, was on a training flight in thick fog when it hit the flagpole on St Phillip's church on Heigham Road, Norwich. The pilot, Second Lieutenant Ralph Dooley, desperately struggled to avoid landing on the houses below and eventually crashed on waste ground near Barker Street. The crew perished, but their heroism in saving civilian lives was recognised by local residents who erected a memorial plaque near the spot.

Major-General William E. Kepner, Commanding General of the United States 8th Air Force, received the honorary freedom of Norwich in 1945, in recognition of his services to the city while in command of the Second Air Division operating from aerodromes near the city.

The Memorial Library – originally formed from £20,000 subscribed by the men of the American 2nd Air Division based in Norfolk in May 1945 – is a unique 'living memorial' to nearly 7,000 young Americans who lost their lives while serving with this division of the US 8th Air Force during the Second World War. Located in The Forum, the library holds a lending collection of over 4,000 books, covering all aspects of American life and culture as well as a specialist collection devoted to the history of the 2nd Air Division.

The Last Regimental Sergeant Major

Between 4–6 May 1944, 2nd Battalion, Norfolk Regiment fought its most bitter engagement of the far eastern war: the Battle of Kohima. The battalion was to lead a group assault on a high point known as GPT Ridge. The fighting was hard but excellent progress was made, through jungle where visibility was rarely more than 5yds; Japanese positions were rushed and overrun with good shooting accounting for large numbers of the enemy losses and casualties for the battalion were light, thanks in no small part to the efforts of Colour Sergeant Bert 'Winkie' Fitt who was commanding the right-forward platoon of 'B' Company. His able handling of his sections resulted in the capture of three enemy bunkers in quick succession and maintained the impetus of the attack. Further advances were made and the final objective was captured but the battle had taken its toll; three officers and nineteen other ranks were killed and six officers and fifty other ranks were wounded.

The following day, 5 May, was reasonably quiet; ration and ammunition parties had a chance to bring up supplies. Still one objective remained, the bunker christened 'Norfolk Bunker' – which dominated the track to the main road – and an attack was mounted at dawn on 6 May. However, the men ran into deadly machine-gun fire from machine-gun posts that had been dug into the hillside and well camouflaged. The platoon commander, Lieutenant Charles Roberts, was killed almost instantly. Colour Sergeant Fitt, seeing Lieutenant Roberts fall, went forward alone and succeeded in destroying the bunker, at the second attempt, with a well-placed grenade. In the next instant, Fitt was caught by a burst of fire that shattered his jaw. He later recounted, 'It felt like a severe punch. I spat out what was left of my teeth and sprayed the foxhole with my light machine gun.' In the hand-to-hand struggle that followed, Fitt managed to kill his enemy with his own bayonet. As he led his men across the top of the enemy position, Fitt witnessed the last, courageous charge of his company commander, Captain Jack Randle. Randle's platoon was pinned down by the intensity of the machine-gun fire. Appreciating that the destruction of this enemy post was imperative if the operation was to succeed, Randle charged the Japanese post single-handed and sacrificed his life blocking the aperture. He was awarded the VC for this selfless act.

After bringing the survivors out after the battle, Colour Sergeant Fitt was met by his commanding officer, the redoubtable Lieutenant Colonel Robert Scott. Fitt recalled: 'I had an old field dressing wrapped around my face, and he said, "They've got you then. Let's have a look."' The medical officer took off the bandage and Colonel Scott laughed and said, 'Well, you never were an oil painting!' Despite his painful injury, Fitt burst out laughing. Fitt was awarded the Distinguished Conduct Medal for his gallantry and went on to be the very last depot regimental sergeant major of the Royal Norfolk Regiment, remaining a well-respected legend among the men. The 2nd Battalion veteran Arthur Storey, who served with him, recalled: 'He was a soldier first and last. Like everybody he liked his beer and a bit of fun but he was a real fighting man. He was the sort of man you'd follow to hell and back. He never asked anyone to do anything he wouldn't do himself.'

V is for Vengeance

The V2 was a long-range rocket known in Germany as the *Vergeltungswaffe 2* ('retaliation weapon'). London was the main target – although 'short falls' of V weapons occurred over much of south-east England – but there were other targets, including the City of Norwich. Operated by Versuchs Artillerie Batterie 444 under the command of Oberst Gerhard Stegmaier, the launch site for the attacks on the city was in a wood near Rijs in south-west Friesland, Holland.

The first V2 that fell on Norfolk crashed into a field near Ranworth at 4.25 p.m. on 26 September 1944, causing a great explosion and crater, and sent a column of smoke 2,000ft into the air. The only casualty was a man who required treatment for shock after the blast. Many more rockets followed, however. In some cases damage was caused, a number of people were injured and there were many narrow escapes, but by some miracle no one was killed in any of the V2 landings on the county and the City of Norwich was never directly hit. The closest that the rockets came to hitting Norwich was when a V2 crashed into the golf course at Hellesdon on 3 October 1944, leaving a crater which was 33ft by 37ft and 12ft deep. Minor damage was caused to around 400 homes in the area between Dereham Road and Boundary Road, and one casualty – an elderly lady – was treated for shock. This was, nevertheless, undoubtedly a sobering near miss.

The last V2 aimed at Norwich fell on a field at Manor Farm, Ingworth, on 12 October, causing minor damage to twenty-four houses and the church. The last V2 to fall on Norfolk was a 'short fall' aimed at London; it crashed at Welborne, near Mattishall, on 26 October 1944. Landing on open ground at 10.12 a.m., the explosion caused minor damage to nearby farm buildings, the local school, about twenty houses, and brought down the telephone wires. Two men were slightly hurt when horses took fright.

Feathered War Heroes

An often forgotten organisation from the Second World War was the National Pigeon Service, which obtained message-carrying birds from British racing pigeon breeders. A number of the birds recorded on the Meritorious Performance List include those bred by Norwich breeders, including H. Leamon of Lawson Road; S. Rowbotham and T. Franklin of Gresham Road, Drayton Estate; and J. Cowles of Beecheno Road, who provided the dark cheq pied cock 'Neilson' (NURP.41.EAN) who was trained at RAF Gillingham and reliably flew missions of distances between 300 and 500 miles over a period of five years. In 1945, Neilson was selected for a very hazardous task and was dropped in the Ruhr Pocket more than 300 miles distant and, after several days' detention, homed successfully.

Camouflage School

During the Second World War, the Assembly House was requisitioned to become a Royal Engineers School of Camouflage under Captain Oliver Messel (1904–78), a pre- and post-war artist who was famous for creating stage sets and designing the interiors of notable buildings and hotels. He enjoyed letting his imagination and inventive skills run wild, disguising military fortifications and pillboxes as haystacks, castles, ruins and even roadside cafes.

The structural alterations inside the beautiful Georgian Assembly House were done with care, and skilled plasterers on the staff used their spare time to repair the plasterwork on the walls and ceilings. Paintwork was also kept in good order and some of the camouflage artists even painted a number of the interior columns in such a way as to make them appear to be made from marble.

A Royal Norfolk Through and Through

In 1945, Norwich man Ted Shepherd was a 22-year-old lance sergeant serving in 1st Battalion, Royal Norfolk Regiment. After making a successful landing with his comrades on D-Day, he fought his way across Holland and was advancing into Germany through the Reichswald Forest when he was sent forward, along with his section, to locate and destroy an enemy machine-gun position. Ted was a tall and powerfully built man, what happened next is recorded in his citation:

> In the assault on the main strongpoint, this NCO led his men forward with the utmost courage and coolness. Heavy small-arms fire was encountered and a mortar was active. As he assaulted the enemy trenches his Sten gun jammed. Confronted by 2 of the enemy, he threw it at them and then leaped after it empty handed into the trench. Sgt. Shepherd seized both by the neck and banged their heads together with such force that they temporarily lost control. He dragged them out, assisted by another member of his section, and using his fists rendered them completely docile. The Platoon, having completed its task, returned with the prisoners.
>
> Sgt Shepherd was later evacuated as it was discovered he had fractured his knuckles while dealing bare-fisted with the enemy. His courage, cool-headedness and leadership were of outstanding quality and an inspiration to his section, which was 75% untried in battle. His control was remarkable throughout, and the success of the whole operation was mainly due to the two actions fought within the framework of the play by this NCOs Section.

Ted was awarded the Military Medal for bravery in the field and was later promoted to company sergeant major, the youngest in 1 Royal Norfolk.

A great character and familiar face as parade marshal for the Norwich and District Branch of the Normandy Veterans Association, when asked what he did to win his medal, Ted typically replied with great wit. 'I saved the lives of 200 men' he would say and, when asked how he did that, his answer was given deadpan – 'I shot the cook'.

IX

3

ROYAL NORWICH

SOME ROYAL VISITS DOWN THE YEARS

Edward I came to see repairs commence upon the cathedral and stayed in Norwich for a number of days in 1278.

Queen Catherine of Aragon and Cardinal Wolsey visited Norwich on 2 March 1520. All the city companies went to greet the queen 'in Puke and Dirke Tawney Liveries' and the city presented her with 100 marks.

HRH James, Duke of York visited the city and was sumptuously entertained on 10 March 1681.

The Prince of Orange visited the city on 27 October 1797.

The Duke and Duchess of York visited Norwich and opened the Castle Museum and Art Gallery on 23 October 1894.

The Prince of Wales – accompanied by the Duke and Duchess of York, Princess Louise and the Marquis of Lorne – visited Norwich on the occasion of the Musical Festival on 7 October 1896.

The Prince and Princess of Wales visited Norwich to open the new Jenny Lind Infirmary on 30 June 1900. They arrived at Trowse by train from Wolferton and, escorted by the 13th Hussars, were driven to Carrow Abbey, where a large and distinguished party had been invited to meet them at luncheon. Afterwards they proceeded to the new infirmary, which the prince declared open. The Princess of Wales then accepted purses in aid of the endowment fund.

King Edward VII paid what was to be his last official visit to Norwich on 25 October 1909. He presented colours and reviewed the 3,000-strong Territorial Force along with a parade of veterans from the Royal Norfolk Veterans Association, and was sung on his way by 11,000 schoolchildren singing from St James' Hill on Mousehold.

When George V visited Norwich and the Royal Show on 28 June 1911, he conferred knighthoods on both Eustace Gurney the Lord Mayor and the Right Honourable Ailwyn Fellowes.

Queen Mary, with Princess Mary, Prince Henry and Prince George, visited Norwich on 12 January 1914.

When Princess Mary was to marry in 1922, she was presented with a pair of court shoes for the occasion made of all-British materials by ex-servicemen and women in the factories of Messrs P. Haldenstein at Norwich.

Queen Mary and the Duchess of York motored from Sandringham to Norwich to attend the morning performance of the Norfolk and Norwich Musical Festival on 31 October 1924. They lunched with the Bishop of Norwich at the Bishop's Palace and called in to visit the headquarters of the Norfolk Federation of Women's Institutes before they left.

Prince Henry (later the Duke of Gloucester) laid the foundation stone of the new children's block at the Norfolk and Norwich Hospital on 31 January 1925.

HRH the Prince of Wales (later Edward VIII) opened Eaton Park on 30 May 1928. In fact the prince came to Norwich on no less than eleven occasions in the 1920s and '30s to open public works projects.

HRH Princess Mary opened Woodrow Pilling Park on 29 May 1929.

Prince George, Duke of Kent, attended the consecration of the War Memorial Chapel at Norwich Cathedral on 3 May 1932.

Queen Mary was given an enthusiastic welcome when she came to Norwich to open the new Queen Alexandra Memorial Nurses' Home at the Norfolk and Norwich Hospital on 15 October 1932.

On 28 May 1938, Queen Elizabeth came to Norwich to reopen the cathedral cloisters after their four years of restoration and unveil statues of the king and herself erected there. It is worthy of note that Her Majesty had paid for the restoration of one of the bays herself.

The new Norwich City Hall was opened by King George VI and Queen Elizabeth on Saturday, 29 October 1938. An unparalleled crowd of many thousands gathered in the Market Place to watch the event.

On 19 November 1939, the statues of King George V and Queen Mary – in the west cloister of Norwich Cathedral – were presented by Sir William Gentle as a memorial of his year in office as High Sheriff of Norfolk and unveiled by Russell Colman, HM lieutenant for Norfolk.

King George VI made a surprise visit to Norwich on 13 October 1942 to meet people affected by and who served through the bombing of the city, travelling to see the bomb damaged areas for himself.

King Peter of Yugoslavia opened a Yugoslav exhibition at Norwich Castle Museum, and visited two factories and the Norwich Services Club on 12 June 1943.

Queen Mary paid an unofficial visit to Norwich Castle Museum on 3 September 1946. She was accompanied by Lady Fermoy and Lady Margaret Wyndham.

King George VI and Queen Elizabeth visited the centenary Royal Norfolk Agricultural Association Show at Keswick Park on 26 June 1947. Over 50,000 people visited the show; almost double the previous gate record for the two-day event.

Queen Elizabeth visited Norwich to open the new east wing of the Church of England training college at Keswick Hall on 24 April 1951.

Princess Elizabeth visited Norwich to open the Festival of Britain fortnight on 18 June 1951.

Princess Margaret visited Norwich on 8 July 1952 to open the new orthopaedic unit at the Norfolk and Norwich Hospital. She was given a great reception and thousands lined the roads as she was driven through the centre of Norwich.

Queen Elizabeth II visited the University of East Anglia on 24 May 1968.

Princess Anne visited Norwich on 14 January 1972 to open the new Norfolk St John Ambulance headquarters on King Street.

The queen visited Norwich on 11 April 1975 to open a new visitor's centre and to commemorate the restoration of the cathedral roof.

The queen and the Duke of Edinburgh visited Norwich as part of her jubilee tour of Great Britain on 11 July 1977.

The queen visited Her Majesty's stationery office on the occasion of the bicentenary of the government office on 30 April 1986.

Princess Anne visited Norwich Castle on 21 April 1988.

Queen Elizabeth, the Queen Mother, came to Norwich to open the Royal Norfolk Regimental Museum at the Shirehall on 20 July 1990.

Queen Elizabeth II came to Norwich to open The Forum on 18 July 2002. During her visit, the queen sent her largest email ever, from the Norfolk and Norwich Millennium Library to 114,000 schoolchildren in 452 schools across Norfolk. She then toured the building with the Duke of Edinburgh, who also visited the 2nd Air Division Memorial Library, before meeting crowds of people outside.

GOOD QUEEN BESS

Queen Elizabeth I visited Norwich during her progress through Suffolk and Norfolk in August 1578. Arriving from Ipswich on horseback, she lodged at the Bishop's Palace and, over a number of days, was entertained with splendid pageantries, watched theatrical performances, dined publicly in the north alley of the cathedral cloister, and had time to go hunting on horseback and watch wrestling and shooting on Mousehold Heath. In preparation for her visit, the houses, streets and lanes were ordered to be repaired and beautified. St Stephen's Gate and the section of city wall where she would be entering the city were renovated, the Market Cross was painted (the posts in timber colour, the rest in white) and the pillory and cage were removed. The churchyard wall at St John Maddermarket was taken down and rebuilt to widen the street.

THE MERRY MONARCH

King Charles II, his queen, and the dukes of York, Monmouth, and Buckingham visited the city on Thursday, 28 September 1671. The party were met at Trowse Bridge by the mayor, with all the regalia, sheriffs, aldermen, common council and militia who had been newly clothed in red, to conduct them to the Duke's Palace, where they lodged and were magnificently entertained by Lord Henry Howard. The next day, the king went to the cathedral, was sung into the church with an anthem and was noted to have kneeled on the hard stone to make his devotion. After being entertained at the Bishop's Palace, the party proceeded to the Guildhall where the king appeared to the people from the balcony and viewed the trained bands drawn up in the Market Place. After this he rode down to the New Hall (St Andrew's Hall) where he was feasted by the city, and knighted the mayor (who earnestly begged to be excused) and the physician and philosopher Thomas Browne, who truly deserved the honour.

Charles II, having received an address from the City of Norwich, commented, 'Certainly the people of Norwich are a very loyal sort of people, or else they are mad.'

QUEEN VICTORIA'S DIAMOND JUBILEE

The city's celebrations of the Diamond Jubilee of Queen Victoria began on Sunday, 20 June 1897 with a special thanksgiving services at the cathedral, St Peter Mancroft and other churches. On the 21st, 125 carcases of sheep and twenty quarters of beef – allotted to Norwich out of the gift sent from Australia for distribution among the poor in the large towns of Great Britain – were divided among 1,500 recipients at Blackfriars' Hall.

The Jubilee day was celebrated on the 22nd. Early in the morning the bells of St Peter Mancroft were rung and a royal salute of twenty-one guns were fired on Mousehold Heath by the mounted batteries of the Artillery Volunteers. Later, 9,000 children from the public elementary schools assembled in the Market Place and sang the national anthem, and Mr George White, chairman of the school board, announced, amid great enthusiasm, that the queen had conferred the honour of knighthood upon the mayor, Mr Charles Gilman. A service of praise and thanksgiving was held at the cathedral at 11 a.m., and was attended in state by the mayor and Corporation. At noon the Artillery and Rifle Volunteers, with the depot company of the Norfolk Regiment, fired a *feu de joie* in the Market Place and, at 1 p.m., Sir Charles and Lady Gilman held a reception at the Guildhall, where the company were invited to drink the queen's health. In the afternoon there was a floral

procession through the streets of the city, sports took place on the Earlham Road Recreation Ground, a costumed cricket match was played on the Lakenham ground, and a captive balloon made frequent ascents from the Cattle Market. In the evening the city was illuminated; a firework display was given on Castle Meadow and a bonfire was lit on St James' Hill. On the 24th, the mayor and sheriff gave a dinner at St Andrew's Hall to upwards of 1,000 of the aged poor, and in the evening Sir Charles and Lady Gilman held a brilliant reception at the Castle Museum.

The children's procession for Queen Victoria's Diamond Jubilee celebrations in Norwich on Tuesday, 22 June 1897 involved about 21,000 children. Every one of them received a Jubilee Medallion with a ribbon and safety pin. The processions were as follows:

• South Heigham District, followed a crimson banner, headed by the Co-operative Band
• Mid-Heigham District, followed a dark blue banner, headed by the St Edmund's Band
• North Heigham District, followed a yellow banner, headed by the Anchor Brewery Band
• St Augustine's District, followed a pink flag, headed by the St George's Works' Band
• St George's District, followed a green flag, headed by the St Andrew's Band
• Pockthorpe District, followed a purple flag, headed by the Norfolk and Norwich Band

The children marched to the Market Place for 9.45 a.m., took up their allotted positions, sang the national anthem 'Rule Britannia' and 'The Old Hundredth' before cheers were given for the queen.

4

CRIME AND PUNISHMENT

LOLLARD'S PIT

The first individuals to be burned for heresy in Lollard's Pit in Norwich were William Wyatt, William Waddon and Hugh Pye in 1427. The first Protestant martyr to be burned there was Thomas Bilney on 19 August 1531; he was followed by many more during the reign of 'Bloody' Queen Mary. The last heretic to be burned at Norwich was John Lewes, who met his end on 18 September 1583 in the castle ditches, having been found guilty of blasphemy.

THE DUCKING STOOL

The ducking or cucking stool, used to dunk common scolds in the Wensum, was situated on Fye Bridge. The court book states that scolds or women of blemished reputation were to be carried 'in a cart with a paper in her hand and a bason tinkling before her and so to the cucking stole and ducked three times in the water'. The stool was removed in the eighteenth century but its name was preserved for many years after in the adjoining row of houses (now demolished), which bore the name of Coke Row, a corruption of the old name of Cokyng (Cucking) Row.

PIN YOUR EARS BACK

Matthew Hamond, a Hethersett wheelwright, was an obstinate heretic and blasphemer. Found guilty of 'reviling the Queen's Majesty and denying the doctrine of the Trinity' he was put in the pillory in Norwich Market Place on 13 May 1578 and both his ears were nailed to the wood. He was burnt alive in the Castle Ditch the following week.

HANGED, DRAWN AND QUARTERED

In 1615, Catholic priest Thomas Tunstall was hanged, drawn and quartered upon the gallows by Magdalen Gate. His head was then set upon a pole on St Benedict's Gate and his quarters displayed upon four other gates of the city.

RIOT!

On 27 September 1766, a dreadful riot occurred in Norwich on account of the great scarcity and price of provisions, especially corn. The houses of bakers were damaged, a large malthouse outside Conesford Gate was burned and a Tombland baker's house was totally destroyed. The riot was quelled by 'magistrates and citizens'. Thirty perpetrators were gathered together and tried as the ringleaders; eight were sentenced to death but only two (John Hall and David Long) actually went to the gallows.

BODYSNATCHERS

Owing to the frequency with which a number of trunks measuring 28in long, 13in wide and 12in deep had been sent from the Rampant Horse Inn by coach to London, suspicion was aroused at the coach office in February 1823. Direction was given that the porter bringing the next trunk should be detained and the item examined. When it was opened, it was found to contain the body of an old man! Revd George Carter identified the man as a Mr Brundall who he had buried a few days earlier and Brundall's grave was found to contain only the coffin and a shroud. From information given by the porter, two men named Collins and Crowe were apprehended and committed for trial at the quarter sessions. They were found guilty and were sentenced to three months' imprisonment and a fine of £50.

THE NORWICH DUMPLING POISONER

John Stratford (42) was a hard-working whitesmith in the city, and produced much of the ironwork for the new Norwich City Gaol. He and his wife had been friends with Thomas and Jane Briggs for about seven years when Stratford became intimate with Jane and she became pregnant as a result, giving birth to his child in June 1828. At around the same time, Jane's husband Thomas was taken into the Norwich Workhouse infirmary after he became bedridden with cancer. Jane regularly bought flour for his diet of 'thick milk' that had to be fed to him. In January 1829, Stratford bought 2oz of arsenic from a local chemist, claiming that he needed it in order to kill some rats. On 11 February, Stratford turned up at the workhouse with a sack of flour marked 'To Thomas Briggs, sick in the workhouse', which he left at the kitchen window and it was put in a cupboard ready for future feeds.

On 2 March, John Burgess – husband to Rhoda, one of Stratford's nurses – used some of Brigg's flour to make dumplings. When they were cooked, Rhoda carried two pieces to her son, came back and ate some of what was left with Mary Moss and Ann Piller. Rhoda rapidly and violently fell sick, as did the others who had partaken of the dumplings. John Burgess was soon taken to his bed and died soon afterwards; his post-mortem revealed evidence of arsenic poisoning. The flour that the dumplings were made from was also found to have arsenic mixed in it. The writing on the bag the flour came in was matched to a sample of Stratford's handwriting and he was taken to trial. Found guilty, Stratford dictated a confession while in the condemned cell and has the dubious honour of being the first man to be executed at the new Norwich City Prison on 17 August 1829.

PRISON BREAK!

Highwaymen John and William Brooks attempted to escape from their cell in Bigod's Tower in Norwich Castle in February 1835. Their improvised rope – made from a blanket and a rug – gave way, causing William Brooks to plummet about 70ft to the ground. Despite his thighs, pelvis, left arm and the ribs on his left side being broken (along with a large swelling which formed on the back of his head), he recovered and was sentenced to transportation for life.

HANGMAN'S RECORD – SOME INFAMOUS LOCAL CRIMES ENDING IN EXECUTION

Frances Billing and Catherine Frary, 'The Burnham Poisoners', were executed in front of Norwich Castle on 10 August 1835. This would prove to be the last public double execution of women in the county. They were also the last women to hang in Norfolk.

James Blomfield Rush, the murderer of Isaac Jermy the Recorder of Norwich and his son Jermy Jermy at Stanfield Hall, was hanged in front of Norwich Castle on 21 April 1849. One of the most notorious and sensational crimes of the nineteenth century, thousands came to see him hang and there was even a special train that brought spectators up from London.

The last public execution in Norfolk was carried out in Norwich on 26 August 1867 by executioner William Calcraft in front of Norwich Castle. Calcraft hanged Hubbard Lingley for the murder of his uncle Benjamin Black at Barton Bendish.

During the execution of wife-killer Robert Goodale by hanging at Norwich Castle Gaol on 30 November 1885, Goodale's head was torn off by the rope. The executioner, James Berry, was acquitted of fault but the incident was known ever after as 'The Goodale Mess'. Charles Mackie, who was present at the execution as a representative of the press, always said with some pride that he was present at 'the last judicial decapitation in Britain'.

The last person to hang at Norwich Castle was George Harmer on 13 December 1886. Harmer had killed Henry Last, an elderly master carver, during a robbery at Last's home in Post Office Tavern Yard, on the corner of School Lane, off Bedford Street.

The first man to hang at the new HM Prison Norwich, off Plumstead Road, was George Watt on 12 July 1898. He was given an appointment with the executioner for shooting his wife Sophia at Denmark Terrace, Sprowston Road, Norwich.

The last execution to be conducted in Norfolk took place at HM Prison Norwich on 19 July 1951 when Dennis Moore and Alfred Reynolds went jointly to the gallows. Although the cases were totally unconnected, both were hanged for the murder of their pregnant girlfriends. The executions were conducted under Albert Pierrepoint, with Syd Dernley as assistant in respect of Moore, and Harry Allen and Robert 'Les' Stewart for Reynolds.

CONSTABULARY DUTIES

The new police (all eighteen of them) went on duty for the first time in Norwich on 1 March 1836. Constables were paid 15*s* a week with a stoppage of 1*s* for clothing – even though they had to provide their own trousers.

The first crime statistics for the new Norwich Police ran from 25 December 1837 until 25 December 1838. These show that the force, over a period of twelve months, dealt with a total of sixty-nine felonies, fifty-six assaults, 113 disorderly persons and five cases of using false coins.

In 1842 there were twenty-four policemen and eight supernumeraries who were appointed by the council and dressed in the same style as the Metropolitan Police. Known as the Day Police, they served under Superintendent Peter Yarrington and a sergeant whose duty was to see that the men attended to their beats. At 11 p.m. they were relieved by the night watch of thirty-eight men, including supernumeraries. They patrolled their beats, some every quarter of an hour, others every half an hour. To ascertain if they were attentive to their duties, registers with clock faces were placed in various houses across the city and each man was provided with a key with which to mark the time of his round. There was also river police with two boats, with one inspector and two men in each boat.

On 23 June 1846, PC William Callow of Norwich City Police was the first Norfolk police officer to die from injuries sustained in the course of his duties after receiving head injuries from an angry mob throwing large stones, bottles and sticks while Callow and a number of his colleagues were escorting refractory paupers from the workhouse on St Andrew's Hill to the Norwich City Gaol.

The Norwich City Police appeared in a new uniform on 9 March 1855. The principal alteration in the clothing was the substitution of a frock coat for the unsightly long-tailed coat. This was considered a far more becoming uniform for a civil force.

When Robert Hitchman resigned from the office of Norwich City Police's chief constable, which he had held for thirty-eight years, he was granted a retiring pension of £273 6*s* 8*d*. His successor, Edwin F. Winch – previously chief constable of Truro – received a salary of £350 per annum.

Norfolk Constabulary amalgamated with Norwich City Police and Great Yarmouth Borough Police to form Norfolk Joint Constabulary in 1968. In 1974, it returned to the name Norfolk Constabulary.

A DARK TALE

In 1842, a human skeleton was recovered from the riverbed at Costessey Mills by a boat owned by Messrs Culley and it was recalled that a Jewish pedlar, known as 'Old Abraham', had mysteriously disappeared some eight years previously. It was also remembered that one Robert Page – who had been sentenced to transportation for life for sheep stealing at Drayton in 1834 – had told his prison warders that if he were taken to Costessey he could show them 'something that would make their hair stand on end' beneath a certain willow tree. Perhaps by a curious coincidence, the skeleton was found beneath a willow which overhung the river. It was stated that the body had been staked down in the bed of the stream …

WITCHCRAFT

On 6 May 1843, Norwich Police Court saw a woman named Kedge complain to the magistrate that another woman, of the name of Clarke, had cursed her and sent her and her children a vast number of vermin. Clarke refuted the claim and alleged that Mrs Kedge was harbouring her (Mrs Clarke's) husband.

It was revealed that Mrs Kedge had given Clarke a small piece of paper, upon which the Lord's Prayer was reproduced in tiny writing, in order to protect herself – asserting that putting the written prayer in the perpetrator's hands would mean that all danger from witchery was over.

THE TABERNACLE STREET HORROR

On 21 June 1851, the first of a number of female body parts were found at a variety of locations around the city. Over the following four weeks of searching, the police collected two hands, two feet, a thigh bone, lower leg bones, parts of a pelvis, some vertebrae and a grisly selection of flesh, including strips of skin and muscle. The portions of flesh were preserved in wine and examined, along with the bones, by a team of local surgeons who concluded that the remains were those of an adult female. However, they were grievously inaccurate in their opinion of her age, which they pronounced as being around 25 years. In the absence of anyone answering such a description being missing from the locale, the body parts were dismissed as a prank set up by medical students and the matter fell from public interest. That is until William Sheward (57) walked into the suburban police station on Carter Street, Walworth, South London on 1 January 1869.

Sheward could no longer live with the guilt of the murder of his wife, Martha. Having failed to take his own life, he handed himself over to the police and confessed he had killed Martha by stabbing her in the throat with his razor during an argument at their home on Tabernacle Street, Norwich. Over the next few days he had disposed of her body by dismembering it and distributing the parts around Norwich. Martha was not instantly missed as her closest family were in Wymondham and she was much older (54) than the age ascribed to the body parts by the surgeons. During later years he managed to fend off enquiries about her from her family by claiming she had run off to London and he had not seen or heard from her for years. Sheward was returned to Norwich and tried before the Norfolk Lent Assizes in March 1869. He was found guilty and executed by William Calcraft within the walls of Norwich City Gaol on 20 April 1869.

A SAD END

John L'Estrange of Union Place, a well-known and published archaeological authority of Norfolk, was brought before the assizes in August 1877, charged with forging the name of Francis Gostling Foster, distributor of stamps, with intent to defraud and with stealing stamps to the amount of £1,400. L'Estrange had been in charge of the stamp department for twenty years. He pleaded guilty, and was sentenced by Sir James Fitzjames Stephen to seven years' penal servitude. L'Estrange later died in Millbank Prison.

MURDER ON THE WALK

Arthur Riches (36), fishhawker, murdered his wife by stabbing her on The Walk in the Haymarket on 8 November 1886. He was tried at Norwich Assizes in November and found guilty, but strongly recommended to mercy on account of the great provocation he had received – his wife having recently moved in with another man. The prisoner was sentenced to death, but the punishment

WIFE MURDER at NORWICH.

was afterwards commuted to penal servitude for life. Riches died at Parkhurst Convict Prison, Isle of Wight, in April 1898.

GAOLS AND GAOLERS

The new prison, built to replace the old Norwich Castle Prison and the old Norwich City Gaol, was opened on Prison Road (now Knox Road) on 16 July 1887.

In 1977, Norwich Prison was one of first seven prisons to employ women officers in men's gaols.

JACK THE RIPPER

Norwich labourer Michael Barker was brought before Norwich Guildhall magistrates in October 1895 after he had grabbed a shovel, smashed glass in Mr Page's pub and then stood in the middle of the street shouting, 'I'm Jack the Ripper!' Arrested by PC Wharton, Barker admitted he was drunk. The court was not convinced by his claim that he was the Ripper and he was fined 10s plus costs or fourteen days in prison.

SUFFRAGETTE INCENDIARY!

When fire broke out in buildings on Storey's Way, Cambridge, on the night of 17 May 1913, rags and paraffin were found and the footprints of a woman were clearly visible in the wet cement of a kitchen floor. Under a broken window, a spot of blood and a woman's gold watch were found. The watch was traced to Miriam Pratt (23), a schoolteacher who lodged on Turner Road with her aunt and uncle, a police sergeant with the Norwich City Police. Miriam was a suffragette, who had said she was going to the East Cambridgeshire election to deliver leaflets. When confronted by her uncle, she confessed that she had been at Storey's Way and had cut herself as she attempted to get the putty out of the window to remove the pane. She revealed that she was with two other women; one was Miss Markham, the other she refused to name.

Miriam Pratt was insistent that she was not the one who started the fire. Nevertheless, at Cambridge Assizes, Miriam's uncle gave evidence against her, she was found guilty of arson and Mr Justice Bray sentenced her to eighteen months in prison. She was not forgotten, however, and the suffragette press extolled her sacrifice for the cause.

In October 1913, Mr Justice Bray, along with the Corporation and local magistracy, attended a service at Norwich Cathedral. During the collection a group of suffragettes rose and chanted the words, 'Lord help and save Miriam Pratt and all those being tortured in prison for conscience sake.' Having finished their recital, the suffragettes resumed their seats. They were not asked to leave the building and after the service they distributed printed accounts of Miss Pratt's defence at the cathedral doors.

GUARDED PAINTINGS

In the immediate aftermath of an axe attack by a suffragette upon the painting known as the *Rokeby Venus* at the National Gallery in London, detectives were present to protect the pictures in St Andrew's Hall during the sitting of the Free Church Council in March 1914. Two of the more valuable pieces of artwork – a Gainsborough and the Beechey portrait of Nelson – were covered in tarpaulin and policemen in plain clothes were posted nearby.

MANHUNT!

A daring escape was made from Norwich Prison by a powerfully built man named Charles Baker (26) on 6 June 1923. Baker was serving a sentence for 'warehouse breaking' and – along with another prisoner – he was working under guard in the governor's house. Using a heavy pickaxe handle, Baker felled warder Lewis Roberts and made his escape by climbing through a window and over a wall on to a public road. Norwich City Police and Norfolk County Constabulary were immediately informed, and soon officers were searching in every direction in motor cars, on bicycles and on foot. A description and a photograph of Baker was circulated across the country. After a few days at large, Baker was recognised and recaptured in Hertford on 12 June 1923.

THE NORWICH FORGER

In 1923, one Thomas Stead (aliases George Harrison, Thomas McKin and T. Curtis), formerly an engraver and designer at the Norwich School of Art, established himself aboard a derelict submarine chaser on the River Yare near Norwich. Here he had a printing press and a forgers plant upon which he printed £1 Bank of England notes ... until he was arrested for the crime. While being handed over by his police escort at the gate of Leicester Gaol in 1924, Stead made a sudden dash for freedom and escaped into the darkness. His description was circulated and a reward of £10 was offered for his capture. Stead's run gained him a total of four months' freedom but he was eventually recaptured, tried and found guilty at Peterborough Quarter Sessions and sentenced to five years' penal servitude.

NO CASES IN THE COURT

When there were no cases to be heard at the Norwich Assizes in June 1924, Mr Justice Sankey and the clerk of assize were each presented with a pair of white gloves.

END OF A CRIME ERA

Infamous East End gangster Reggie Kray was serving the last period of his sentence at Wayland Prison in Norfolk. He was released on compassionate grounds as a result of cancer, and died on 1 October 2000 at the Town House Hotel in Thorpe St Andrew, Norwich.

GREAT TRAIN ROBBERY

The notorious 'Great Train Robber' Ronnie Biggs was moved from Belmarsh Prison to Norwich Prison in July 2007 until his release on compassionate grounds in 2009. He died in 2013.

5

NORWICH PEOPLE, FAMOUS AND NOT SO

Matthew Parker, theologian and one of the primary architects of the *Thirty-Nine Articles* (the defining statements of Anglican doctrine), was born in Norwich in 1504. Parker served as Archbishop of Canterbury from 1559 until his death in 1575.

John Caius was born in Norwich in October 1510 and went on to become president of the College of Physicians nine times and physician to Edward VI, Queen Mary and Queen Elizabeth. His greatest legacy, however, was becoming the second founder of the present Gonville and Caius College, Cambridge.

William Cuningham MD was born in Norwich in 1531 and lived in the city. In 1559, he published his *Cosmographical Glass*, which contained the first description of the city attempted with a bird's-eye map engraved by Cuningham himself.

Robert Greene, dramatist and author of the comedy *Friar Bacon and Friar Bungay*, was born in Norwich in 1558.

Sir Thomas Browne (1605–82), physician and philosopher, was the author of *Religio Medici* (*Religion of a Physician*), the first defence and contemplation of the medical profession in modern literature. He also produced a number of other books on religion, science and the esoteric. Browne spent most of his life in Norwich.

Francis Blomefield (1705–51), author of *The History of Norfolk*, lived for a number of years on Willow Lane, St Giles.

John Bruckner (1726–1801), the Lutheran divine, settled in the city as a preacher at the French church in 1753.

Sir John Fenn (1739–94), best known as the editor of the Paston Letters, was born in Norwich in 1739 and served as the High Sheriff of Norfolk in 1791–92.

Richard Beatniffe (1740–1818), the local author of *Norfolk Tour*, saw his work go through six editions before he died.

Anna Laetitia Barbauld (1743–1825), children's author and 'woman of letters', lived in Norwich for a number of years. Her books *Lessons for Children* and *Hymns in Prose for Children* were a revolution in children's literature because the needs of the child reader were seriously considered in them for the very first time. The language that she used was a simple dialogue and she demanded that her books be printed in large type with wide margins so that children could easily read them.

Olaudah Equiano (1745–97), freed slave and tireless campaigner for the abolition of slavery, came to Norwich in 1794 and stayed for a number of months, giving lectures and attending local events. He was given a warm welcome, received huge support for the abolition cause, and many more subscribers came forward for his book and the eighth edition of his autobiography *The Interesting Narrative of the Life of Olaudah Equiano, or Gustavus Vassa, the African*, which was printed in Norwich.

James Hooke, born in Norwich in 1746, was the son of a razor grinder and cutler. He was a celebrated organist and the composer of more than 2,400 songs, 149 complete works or operas, one oratorio and numerous odes and anthems. His most popular work was 'The Lass of Richmond Hill'.

Luke Hansard (1752–1828) was the man who printed the *Journals of the House of Commons* from 1774 until his death in 1828, and whose legacy remains in the name of the record of Parliamentary debate – was born in St Mary's parish, Norwich, in 1752.

Sir William Beechey (1753–1839), this eminent portrait painter resided in Norwich between 1782 and 1787 and went on to paint four of the works for the civic portrait collection that hang in St Andrew's and Blackfriar's Halls.

Admiral Lord Horatio Nelson (1758–1805), Britain's greatest naval commander, attended King Edward VI Grammar School in Norwich before he went to the Paston School in North Walsham.

Sir James Edward Smith MD, botanist, founder and first president of the Linnaean Society, was born at Norwich in 1759.

Anne Plumptre (1760–1818), fiction and travel writer and translator, as well as an active member of the Enfield circle of literati, was born and died in Norwich. One of the first to introduce German plays to London, she translated many of the dramas of Kotzebue in 1798 and 1799. Miss Plumptre resided in France between 1802 and 1805. During this time she became an ardent admirer of Napoleon, to the degree that in 1810 she declared that she would welcome him if he invaded England because he would do away with the aristocracy and give the country a better government.

James Bennett (1760–1845) had a long career as a watch and clockmaker, which he commenced at the age of 13 with a seven-year apprenticeship to Peter Amyot. Bennett invented an instrument for performing the operation of the trepan and was also recorded to be the first man to make an electrical machine in Norwich. He died at his house near St Giles Gates.

Frank Sayers MD (1763–1817) author of *Poems, Containing Sketches of the Northern Mythology* and a volume of *Disquisitions, Metaphysical and Literary*, died at his house in the Lower Close, aged 55.

James Sillett (1764–1840) was renowned for his skill in depicting game, fruit and flowers in miniature. He spent most of his life in Norwich and died there on 6 May 1840.

Elizabeth Bentley (1767–1839) was born and lived in Norwich. Her first book, *Genuine Poetical Compositions, on Various Subjects*, was published in Norwich by a subscription of almost 2,000 people in 1791.

John Crome (1768–1821), founder of the Norwich School of Painters, was born the son of a weaver in the city. Having demonstrated an aptitude for painting, he was apprenticed to Francis Whistler – a Norwich house, coach and sign painter – before he made his reputation as a landscape artist of remarkable quality. Often using the landscape immediately around Norfolk as his subject, Crome's works are now held in major art collections around the world, including the Tate in London and the Metropolitan Museum of Art in New York. He is buried in St George's church, Colegate.

Robert Ladbrooke (1768–1842), an artist and engraver who artistically and loyally captured much of Norfolk in the first half of the nineteenth century, died at his home on Scole's Green, Norwich, on 11 October 1842, aged 73.

Amelia Opie (1771–1853), a society socialite, novelist and poet known as 'The Gay Quaker', was born in Norwich in 1771. Her first novel, *The Dangers of Coquetry*, was published when she was just 18 years old. Amelia died at her home on Castle Meadow and was buried in the Gildencroft Quaker cemetery, Norwich.

Commander Robert Tinkler (1774–1820) was a cabin boy on board the *Bounty*, who at the time of the infamous mutiny in 1789, was one of the twelve turned adrift with Captain Bligh. He was present aboard HMS *Isis* as part of Lord Nelson's squadron at the Battle of Copenhagen in 1801 and later rose to the rank of post-captain and commander. He died in Norwich on 15 August 1820 and was buried in St Margaret's churchyard in St Benedict's Street.

William Crotch, born in Norwich in 1775, was a child prodigy in music, who played before George III whilst only 3½ years old. He went on to be appointed Professor of Music at St John's College, Oxford where he taught for fifty years.

John Hunt (1777–1842) a Norwich engraver and author of *British Ornithology*, published this three-volume work between 1815 and 1822. It was one of the earliest and most ambitious attempts to describe and illustrate the wild bird species of the nation.

Elizabeth Fry (née Gurney) was born in Gurney Court, off Magdalen Street in Norwich, on 21 May 1780. A Quaker and Christian philanthropist, she promoted social reform and worked to raise awareness of the terrible conditions found in prisons.

Hannah Sarah Hancock (1781–1850), who compiled a dictionary for children when she was just 8 years old, was born at St Helen's, Norwich.

John Sell Cotman (1782–1842), probably the most famous of the Norwich School of Painters, was born in Norwich and retained his links with the city and county for the rest of his life. He joined the Norwich Society of Artists, was made president of the society in 1811, and showed his works at many of their annual exhibitions over the years. There are over 2,000 pieces of his work in the Norwich Castle Museum and Art Gallery collection as well as in prominent galleries across Britain and America.

Sarah Ann Glover (1785–1867) was born in The Close and lived in Norwich for many years. While in the city she created the Tonic Sol-fa, a pedagogical technique for teaching sight-singing (e.g. do, reh, me, fa, so, la, te, do).

Sir Thomas Fowell Buxton (1786–1845), who led the Parliamentary campaign responsible for the 1833 Act that freed 700,000 slaves then held in the West Indies and elsewhere in the British Empire, was no stranger to Norwich. He worked with Elizabeth Fry to promote prison reform and spoke at the Friends Meeting House and St Andrew's Hall to raise awareness for his causes.

Samuel Woodward (1790–1838), a geologist and antiquary, was author of such books as *A Synoptical Table of British Organic Remains* (1830), which was the first work of its kind in Britain, and *An Outline of the Geology of Norfolk* (1833).

John Dalrymple, an early opthalmologist, was born in Norwich in 1803. He is best known for his histological work with Henry Bence Jones in the discovery of the albumin that became known as the Bence Jones protein.

James Brooke (1803–68), the first White Rajah of Sarawak, received a brief education at the grammar school in Norwich, from which he ran away.

George Borrow (1803–81), the celebrated traveller and the author of *The Bible in Spain*, *Lavengro* and *The Romany Rye*, resided in a house on Willow Lane in Norwich during the early period of his life. Arthur Michael Samuel MP presented the house to the Corporation of the City of Norwich when he was Lord Mayor in 1913. The generosity of Mr W.T.F. Jarrold and other Borrovians saw the house furnished in the style of the period and opened to the public. Sadly Borrow House is no longer a museum to the great man.

Giovanni Bianchi (*c.* 1808–72) was an Italian figurinai maker who worked on St George's Middle Street for thirty years. However, he was best known among the phrenology societies around the country for the plaster casts he supplied to them for study, taken so skilfully from the heads of dead distinguished and brilliant men, as well as the heads of executed criminals at Norwich Castle, such as James Rush, the infamous Stanfield Hall Murderer.

Henry Rowe was born in Norwich in 1812 and ran away from home to join a company of strolling players when he was 19. Rowe ended up as a regular member of the famous Lyceum Company under Sir Henry Irving from 1881 until his death in 1896.

Augustus Jessopp (1823–1914), academic, antiquarian and author of a number of volumes including *The Coming of the Friars*, *Arcady for Better or Worse* and *The Trials of a Country Parson*, was headmaster of King Edward VI Grammar School in Norwich and Rector of Scarning for thirty-two years. He will probably be best remembered, however, for his published description of an encounter with a ghost at Mannington Hall in 1879.

Joseph Wiggins, born in Norwich in 1832, was a mariner and navigator who demonstrated the practicality of sea-based trade between countries bordering on the North Sea and the northern portion of Siberia.

William Childerhouse, born in 1841, held the office of Norwich bellman from 1877 until his death. In a world before radio or television, bellmen or criers were essential broadcasters in every city and town. Using his stentorian voice and wielding his 10lb bell, it was estimated that over the years he had cried 600,000 announcements and walked a total of 70,000 miles. His Corporation salary gave him 13*s* 4*d* per annum with £5 a year for civic sword bearing and toast mastering at banquets.

Walter Rye (1843–1929), best known as a Norwich and Norfolk antiquarian, was, in his youth, a noted sportsman who held over 100 prizes for walking, running and cycling and was known as the 'father' of paper chase cross-country running (where 'hares' left a trail of paper for the 'hounds' who were chasing them). In 1868, he held all world walking records from 1 mile to 7 miles. Rye practiced as a solicitor from 1866 until his retirement in 1900. He was the founder and honorary solicitor of the Norfolk Broads Protection Society, and also the author of several works on the Broads. Settling at his lovely home at No. 66 Clarendon Road, Rye was highly esteemed in Norwich and was made mayor in 1908–09.

As an antiquary, Rye was both able and industrious; he compiled and published over eighty indexes (handbooks mostly relating to Norfolk topography and pedigrees) and possessed a valuable collection of Norfolk manuscripts and documents, which he bequeathed to the City of Norwich. He also spent a small fortune rescuing historically important buildings from destruction by acquiring or helping to acquire properties such as the Maid's Head Hotel, Anguish's House, Bacon's House in Colegate, and Lazar House on Sprowston Road.

Emma Sandys (1843–77), a remarkable artist who captured female beauty in the style of the Pre-Raphaelites, lived most of her life in Norwich. Her father, the Pre-Raphaelite painter, illustrator and draughtsman Augustus Sandys (1829–1904), was also born and lived in the city.

Miss Catherine Maude Nichols – the daughter of W.P. Nichols, a former Mayor of Norwich – was born in the city in 1847. A painter and etcher, Catherine had very little training but worked hard in both British and continental galleries. She painted in oils but made her greatest mark as an etcher and was the first female fellow of the Royal Society of Painter Etchers. Catherine was also a member of the International Union of Fine Arts and regularly exhibited at the Royal Academy, the Salon, the Painter-Etchers in Venice and Melbourne. As an etcher, she produced over 200 plates, a number of them depicting Norwich and Norfolk. Her books also expressed her love and feeling for the county, among them *Old Norwich*, *Cromer Sketches* and *Two Norfolk Idylls*. She died in Norwich in January 1923.

Mary Mann, born in Norwich in 1848, was a prolific Victorian novelist whose career spanned thirty-five years. Moving to Shropham after her marriage, she set many of her fictional stories in the county and drew inspiration from what she saw around her. Although her stories were fictional, her depiction of the hardships of country folk was all too real. Described by some as 'Norfolk's Thomas Hardy', Mann was much admired by D.H. Lawrence. Her books include *The Parish of Hilby* (1883) and *The Fields of Dulditch* (1902).

John Coates Carter (1859–1927), best known for his Arts and Crafts style design and restoration work in churches in South Wales, was born in Norwich. His biggest construction project was Caldey Abbey. At the time of building it was described as 'the greatest phenomenon in the Anglican community at the present time' and today it is considered to be the most complete example of the Arts and Crafts style in the country.

'Billy Bluelight' remains one of the most famous Norwich characters of all time. His real name was William Cullum and he was born on one of the poorer streets of the city in about 1860. He received no formal education but taught himself to read and worked for a number of years at Caley's chocolate factory. Billy was never known for his academic prowess, but he was a fantastic runner and would race against the riverboats (such as the SS *Jenny Lind*) as they travelled from Foundry Bridge in Norwich to Great Yarmouth. On the boat's return journey he would hold his cap out at the end of the gangplank for people to show their appreciation with a small donation. Now, some say he had a bicycle or two stashed along the route but the passengers certainly saw him running along the riverbank for long sections of the journey. Either way, with his merry rhyme – 'My name is Billy Bluelight, my age is forty-five, I hope to get to Carrow bridge before the boat arrive' – Billy certainly made the journey under his own steam for many a year and for years after he was 45. Billy passed away in 1949 but remains a fondly remembered Norwich personality; there is even a sculpture of him at Wherryman's Way, Bramerton.

James Frederick 'Fred' Henderson (1867–1957), Socialist writer and Labour Party politician, was born in Norwich and founded a branch of the Socialist League in the city in 1886. The following year, Henderson was imprisoned for four months after being found guilty of incitement to riot when groups of unemployed workers looted food shops. Henderson is believed to have been one of the last men set to work on the treadmill before it was abolished in British prisons. Upon his release, Henderson carried on in politics and, after a few years away in London, returned to Norwich where in 1902 he became the first socialist to be elected to the City Council. In 1923 he was elected alderman and was thus a member of the council until his death. Henderson also served as Lord Mayor in 1939–40 and was granted the freedom of the city in 1947.

Edgar Thomas Larner (1869–1930), radio and television experimenter and pioneer, was born in Norwich. He wrote a number of books and manuals on such topics as *Radio and Frequency Currents* (1923), *Valve Sets: Construction and Maintenance* (1925) and *Practical Television, etc.* (1928), the latter including a foreword by his close friend John Logie Baird, the man credited as the innovator and inventor of the world's first television.

Dr Sydney Long (1870–1939), nature conservation pioneer and founder of the Norfolk Naturalists' Trust, lived on Surrey Street in Norwich for many years. The trust was established in 1926 to purchase Cley Marshes. Now known as the Norfolk Wildlife Trust, they maintain sixty nature reserves covering nearly 10,000 acres of coast, heath, marsh and fen in the county.

Sir Arthur Michael Samuel (1872–1942) was the first Jewish Lord Mayor of Norwich. He served from 1912–13 and did much to help alleviate the suffering of Norwich people during the floods of August 1912. In 1918, he was elected as the Member of Parliament for Farnham, a seat he would hold until 1937, and served under Stanley Baldwin as Secretary for Overseas Trade from 1924–27. Samuel was made an Honorary Freeman of Norwich in 1928. He was created Baronet of Mancroft in 1932 and raised to the peerage, choosing the title 1st Baron Mancroft of Mancroft to mark his links to the city.

Sir Alfred Munnings (1878–1959), one of England's finest painters of horses, was born just over the border at Mendham in Suffolk. He moved to Norwich aged 14 to take up a position as apprentice to Page Brothers, the Norwich lithographers, creating posters and advertisements, and studied at the Norwich School of Art in the evenings. Some of Munnings' earliest commissions came from Shaw Tomkins, manager of Caley's and one of Page Brothers' most important customers, who commissioned Munnings to design posters and boxes for chocolates.

Daisy Ashford (1881–1972) wrote the best-selling novella *The Young Visiters* – a romance of high-society love seen through the nursery keyhole – when she was just 9 years old (it was published a few years later in 1919). Ashford wrote other books but none enjoyed the same success as her first. She moved to Reepham in later life and retired to Hellesdon where she died on 15 January 1972.

Ralph Hale Mottram (1883–1971), novelist and local historian, was born in Norwich and was, for many years, the literary doyen of the city. His is best remembered for his *Spanish Farm Trilogy* (1927) based on his experiences as a young officer on the Western Front during the First World War. The trilogy comprised *The Spanish Farm*; *Sixty-Four, Ninety-Four* and *The Crime at Vanderlynden's*. It was later made into a film called the *Roses of Picardy*.

Vernon Castle was born William Vernon Blyth, the son of a publican in Norwich, in 1887. With his American wife, Irene, the pair became world-famous ballroom dancers who appeared on Broadway in such shows as *The Sunshine Girl* (1913) and *Watch Your Step* (1914), which boasted Irving Berlin's first score, written for the Castles. They also starred in the silent film *The Whirl of Life* (1915) and are credited with reviving the popularity of modern dancing.

Richard Hearne, the affectionately remembered television children's entertainer best known for his stage and television character 'Mr Pastry', was born on Lady Lane in Norwich in 1908 and made his stage debut at the Theatre Royal, aged just 6 weeks old.

Sir John Mills (1908–2005), an Oscar-winning actor and star of over 100 feature films, including such classics as *In Which We Serve* (1942), *Great Expectations* (1946), *The Colditz Story* (1954), *Above Us The Waves* (1955), *Ice Cold In Alex* (1958) and *Ryan's Daughter* (1970), attended the Norwich High School for Boys. He didn't much like it and would claim, as one of his achievements there, that he broke the nose of the school bully. He also had football trials with Norwich City Football Club in the 1920s before moving into acting.

Alan Breeze (1909–80), the singer famous for his appearances on the *Billy Cotton Band Show* and notably his rendition of 'I've Got a Lovely Bunch of Coconuts', died at the West Norwich Hospital, aged 71.

Edward Seago, born in Norwich in 1910, was a self-taught artist whose watercolour and oil landscapes received national acclaim and was collected by Queen Elizabeth, the Queen Mother. Ted Seago's paintings were published in a number of books reflecting the travels and experiences of the author, among them were: *Circus Company* (1933); *The Country Scene* (1936), containing forty-two paintings to accompany John Masefield's poetry; *Caravan* (1937); *Peace in War* (1943); *High Endeavour* (1944); *Tideline* (1948); and *With Capricorn to Paris* (1956).

Bernard Meadows (1915–2005), part of the modernist 'geometry of fear' school of British sculptors, was born in Norwich. Meadows' best-known work in the city, entitled *Public Sculpture*, is a controversial assembly of stone blocks and balls of dripping metal with large dimples. It was commissioned for the *Eastern Daily Press* in 1968 and still dominates the frontage of Prospect House, Norwich.

Jimmy Hanley, born in Norwich in 1918, is best known for his roles as a child actor. He also appeared in a number of classic films such as *Boys Will Be Boys* (1935), *Gaslight* (1940), *The Way Ahead* (1944) and *The Blue Lamp* (1950). He is the father of actress Jenny Hanley.

Miss Maude Harwood of St Swithin's Terrace was awarded a Carnegie Hero Trust Certificate in January 1927 and was presented with a cheque for £10 for the bravery she showed in stopping a runaway horse in a crowded Norwich street.

Jack Cohen, a reproductive biologist who is also known for his popular science books and science fiction collaborations – notably *The Science of Discworld* volumes with Terry Pratchett and Ian Stewart – was born in Norwich in 1933.

Frederick Forsyth CBE (born 1938), best known for writing thrillers, including *The Day of the Jackal*, *The Odessa File* and *The Fourth Protocol*, spent three and a half years working for the *Eastern Daily Press*, first in Norwich and then in King's Lynn.

Michael Brunson, distinguished television political reporter and the political editor of ITN in 1986–2000, was born in Norwich in 1940.

Peter Jay Miller, probably best known for his music career as Peter Jay in Peter Jay and the Jaywalkers, was born in Norwich in 1942. What is not widely known is that he released one of the first English psychedelic songs 'Cold Turkey' as Big Boy Pete in 1966, which placed his name in the Rock and Roll Hall of Fame.

Ruth Madoc, best known for her portrayal of bossy holiday camp yellowcoat Gladys Pugh in the hit comedy series *Hi-De-Hi* (1980–88), was actually born in Norwich in 1943 but obtained her lovely Welsh accent after spending most of her childhood with her Welsh grandmother and English grandfather in Llansamlet, Swansea.

Philip Pullman, best known as the best-selling author of the *His Dark Materials* trilogy of fantasy novels, was born in Norwich on 19 October 1946.

Keith Simpson, a prominent military historian and Member of Parliament, was born in Norwich in 1949.

Professor Sir Paul Nurse was born in Norwich in 1949 and was educated at the University of East Anglia. He won the 2001 Nobel Prize in Physiology or Medicine and was President of the Royal Society in 2010.

Ed Balls, the Labour Party MP, was born in Norwich in 1967.

Cathy Dennis, multi-Grammy award-winning singer and songwriter, was born in Norwich in 1969 and studied at Taverham High School. Although she did have a few UK Top 20 hits in her solo career as a singer, her greatest successes have been as a writer. She co-wrote Kylie Minogue's worldwide hit *Can't Get You Out of My Head* along with Rob Davis in 2001 and wrote the hit song *Toxic* for Britney Spears, which won the Grammy for Best Dance Recording. Dennis also had a string of hits with a number of singles she wrote for S Club 7 and a host of international artists. She has penned eight UK Number 1 tracks to date and won five Ivor Novello Awards. In 2004, she was 66th in the *Q Magazine* list of the top 100 most influential people in music.

Jon Tickle, *Big Brother 4* competitor and *Brainiac* co-presenter, was born in Norwich in 1974.

6

NORWICH
AT WORK

WEAVING AND SPINNING

Wool and the weaving trade was a staple industry in Norfolk, from
the Middle Ages until the Industrial Revolution when the power
looms of the North took trade away from the county. The Jacquard
Loom was introduced in Norwich in about 1833 and manufacturers
were able to invent several new fabrics. By 1842 the principle
fabrics made in Norwich were fillover or 'Norwich' shawls, crapes,
challis, plain and fingered poplins, *mousseline de laine* and a then
new fabric called Parmatta cloth introduced by Messrs Willett,
which nearly superseded the use of bombazines for mourning.
The manufacturing of *gros de Naples* and bandana handkerchiefs
was also introduced.

In 1842, Norwich Yarn Company employed over 300 people, had
a 50hp engine and fifty spinning frames in their mill in St Edmund's
and had another establishment near Whitefriar's Bridge. There were
two further yarn mills, one at Lakenham and another on King Street,
which were employed in spinning mohair yarn. Mr Geary's factory
on St Augustine's employed many hands winding cotton on to reels.
Hundreds of Norwich people were employed as piecework weavers
working in their own homes. The rate of wages were between 8*s* and
10*s* to 14*s* and 21*s* a week. Women could earn the same rates while
children were lucky to receive 2*s* 6*d* a week.

JARROLD'S

Jarrold's was founded in 1770 as a drapers and grocers in Woodbridge, Suffolk. In 1815, the business expanded into printing and they took over their first premises in Norwich in 1823, selling books and stationary before moving their printing works to the site in 1830. A nineteenth-century advert states they were 'printers, binders, fancy stationers, die sinkers and engravers' and they maintain a fine reputation for printing at their works in the historic St James Mill to this day. Occupying part of their present site from as early as 1840, the present department store in Norwich was designed by George Skipper and built in 1903–05. The Jarrold stores, always synonymous with a touch of class and good quality, remain in family hands.

THE OLD NORWICH BANKING FIRM

Messrs Gurneys and Co. was founded by John and Henry Gurney, the sons of John Gurney, who earned the title of the 'Weavers' Friend', by reason of his advocacy of their cause. In addition to their ordinary trade as merchants, the Gurney brothers carried on a banking business, first in Pitt Street in 1775, and afterwards in Magdalen Street. In 1779 the Gurneys devoted themselves exclusively to banking and the business was transferred to Bartlett Gurney (son of Henry Gurney), who removed to a premises on Bank Plain with his uncle, John Gurney of Earlham Hall, as a partner. Bartlett Gurney died in 1803 and John Gurney was left sole proprietor, being joined shortly by his cousins, Richard and Joseph Gurney. By the 1870s, Gurney's was the largest private banking house in the provinces. In 1896, Gurney's Bank merged with Backhouse's Bank of Darlington and Barclays Bank of London (along with several other provincial banks controlled by Quaker families), to form what is today known simply as Barclays Bank.

NORWICH SHAWLS

Alderman John Harvey is credited with the introduction of shawl manufacture in Norwich in the 1780s (although some sources suggest that this accolade should actually be attributed to yarn factor Edward Barrow). The product itself was greatly improved by Mr Knights, who commenced making the shawl in silk and worsted; the outline of the pattern being printed, while the flower was embroidered with the needle.

I. W. CALEY & Co.,

SILK MERCERS & SHAWLMEN,

By Special Appointments to H.M. The Queen, The Princess of Wales and the Princess Christian,

NORWICH,

HAVE ALWAYS A WELL-ASSORTED STOCK OF THE MOST

FASHIONABLE SILKS & DRESS FABRICS.

COSTUMES IN THE NEWEST DESIGNS.

PLUSH, SILK AND OTHER MANTLES, SEALSKIN COATS AND FURS.

Orders for Dressmaking stylishly and promptly executed.

A CONSTANT SUPPLY OF THE LATEST PARISIAN MILLINERY.   LADIES' & CHILDREN'S UNDERCLOTHING IN ALL ITS BRANCHES.

THE HOUSEHOLD DEPARTMENT IS ALSO REPLETE WITH THE BEST MAKES IN DAMASK TABLE LINEN, SHEETINGS, QUILTS, FLANNELS, CALICOS, ETC.

Mourning Orders tastefully and expeditiously executed.

FUNERALS ENTIRELY FURNISHED AND CONDUCTED TO ANY DISTANCE.

The heyday of Norwich shawls was in the 1840s and '50s when a working couple could earn as much as £15 a week. There were at least twenty-eight manufacturers producing shawls in the city at this time. One firm, E. & F. Hinde, made no less than twenty-six different types of shawl, representing a total of 39,000 shawls for one year. Norwich shawls were always highly prized for their bright colours and fine designs but the trade was not to last forever and by the 1860s they were fast falling out of fashion and only a few firms manufacturing shawls in the city survived into the twentieth century.

NORWICH UNION

Norwich Union was founded in 1797 when merchant and banker Thomas Bignold formed the Norwich Union Society for the Insurance of Houses, Stock and Merchandise from Fire, later known as the Norwich Union Fire Insurance Office. After a severe winter that caused widespread suffering and loss of life, Bignold also established the Norwich Union Life Insurance Society in 1808. By the early twentieth century, Norwich Union societies were operating worldwide and in 1925, the two Norwich Union companies were brought together when the Life Society bought the entire share capital of the Fire Society. After a number of mergers, Norwich Union is now part of the Aviva Group.

THE MUSTARD KING

Colman's of Norwich can trace its roots back to 1814 when flour miller Jeremiah James Colman took over a mustard manufacturing business at Stoke Holy Cross. Jeremiah took his adopted nephew James into partnership in 1823 and the firm of J. & J. Colman was created. The business grew and acquired larger premises at Carrow in 1856 where new, more efficient production methods were introduced. The Colman's were also benevolent, building a subsidised school for the children of their employees in 1857. They also appointed one of the very first industrial nurses and even established one of the first works canteens in the city. Realising the importance of product visibility, they introduced their distinctive mustard-yellow packaging in 1866 and that same year were granted a special warrant as manufacturers to Queen Victoria. By the early twentieth century, Colman's employed over 3,000 Norwich citizens in mustard, starch and corn flour production. The Colman's brand was purchased by Unilever in 1995.

Another product once made by Colman's at the Carrow Works was starch – used for stiffening collars and cuffs in the late nineteenth and early twentieth centuries. Norwich starch was manufactured entirely from rice grown in the Madras and Bengal presidencies of India. The Colman's site had three warehouses dedicated to the product, each one able to hold 1,000 tons of packed starch. The staff in the starch works numbered about 1,200 and roughly half were women and girls.

THE NORWICH BREWING INDUSTRY

Brewing in Norwich can be traced back centuries; during the eighteenth century, larger-scale breweries began to emerge and by 1836, twenty-seven breweries were recorded in the city. When the railway arrived in Norwich, the brewing industry flourished as breweries were able to send their wares across the county and further afield. By the 1920s, four big breweries dominated the business in Norwich: Morgans, Steward and Patteson, Young's Crawshay & Youngs and Bullard's. Further takeovers forced the demise of brewing in Norwich when the last breweries came under the control of just one company, Watney Mann, in the 1970s. Small-scale independent brewing continues in Norwich but there are no large breweries left in the city today.

Brewers

To the Late King George V.

Steward & Patteson
Ltd.

NORWICH

Established - 1793

Brewers,   Wine   and   Spirit   Merchants

ALL

ALES and STOUT

BREWED FROM

ENGLISH MALT & HOPS

Branches :

GT. YARMOUTH   KING'S LYNN   IPSWICH

EYE

BARNARDS LTD, NORWICH

Charles Barnard, an ironmonger, oil and colourman in Norwich in 1826, entered into a partnership with John Bishop in 1846. Their business grew and soon they occupied premises in St George's and Coslany Street, before they moved again to St Michael's Coslany where they erected the Norfolk Ironworks. The company made its name inventing and manufacturing the original galvanised wire netting and slow combustion stoves. Their reputation, however, was made on their vast range of wrought and cast-iron products, especially fireplaces, and they obtained a royal warrant as makers of iron gates and railings 'By Appointment' to both George V and George VI, as well as providing many supplies for the military in both world wars. Barnards developed their business into a factory on Mousehold from the 1920s. They concentrated on the production of wire-fencing products from the 1950s but, after a number of takeovers, the business finally closed its doors in Norwich in 1991.

CALEY'S

In 1857, A.J. Caley established himself as a chemist on London Street in Norwich. He began making mineral waters in his cellar in 1863 and the business took off before moving to larger premises on the same street. Caley's son Edward joined the business in 1878 and they took over their first building on Chapelfield. In 1883, Caley's began manufacturing cocoa and went from strength to strength, enjoying patronage from both the royal family and the House of Commons. They erected a purpose-built factory, became a joint stock company in 1890 and started making crackers in 1897 as well.

The business remained in the hands of the Caley family until 1918, when it was purchased by the African and Eastern Trade Corporation who sold the firm to John Mackintosh & Sons Limited ('The Yorkshire Toffee King') for £138,000 in 1932. After a further takeover by Rowntree and finally Nestle, the chocolate factory that filled the city air with its warm and tempting smell was closed in 1994 and the Chapelfield shopping mall has been built in its place. The Caley name has been revived by a smaller company that still maintains the best traditions of Caley chocolates. Yummy!

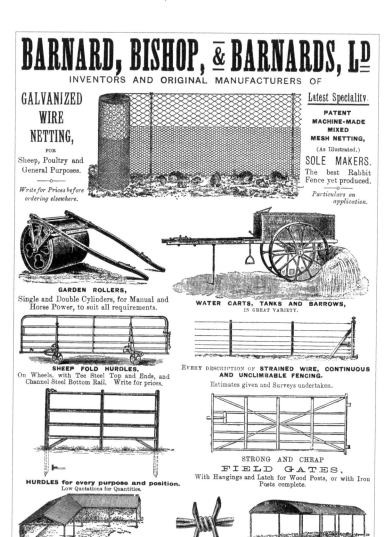

BOULTON & PAUL

Established Norwich ironmonger and foundry owner William Staples Boulton made his manager, Mr J.J. Dawson Paul, a partner in the business in 1869 and renamed the firm Boulton & Paul. At their Rose Lane Works they made all manner of iron products, from hand implements and fencing to building furniture. By 1900, the firm had expanded to further premises on King Street and were supplying their products all over the world. Their greatest challenge, however, came during the First World War when the government asked them to start making aeroplanes. Constructing an airfield on the old cavalry drill ground on Mousehold Heath, their first aircraft was completed and awaiting its test in October 1915, and, by the end of the war, Boulton & Paul had built 2,530 military aircraft. The pressures of war production saw Boulton & Paul move to a 14-acre site soon known as Riverside Works.

After the war, the company were awarded the contract to construct parts for the R101 airship. These parts were manufactured at Norwich and then sent to the airship base at Cardington for assembly. During the Second World War, the Boulton & Paul works in Norwich produced a huge variety of items, from Morrison air-raid shelters to tank transporters and noses for Horsa gliders; continuing their efforts despite being bombed on more than one occasion. By the 1980s, the firm was in decline and the Riverside Works closed in 1986. It was demolished and the site is now occupied by the Riverside shopping, leisure and residential area.

READ ALL ABOUT IT!

In 1895 an amazing array of newspapers were being published in Norwich:

- *Daylight*, published on Saturdays by Edward Burgess, printer, St Stephen's Street
- *Eastern Evening News*, Norfolk News Company, Nos 5–7 Exchange Street
- *Eastern Daily Press*, Norfolk News Company, Nos 5–7 Exchange Street
- *Eastern Weekly Press*, published Friday for Saturday, Norfolk News Company, Nos 5–7 Exchange Street
- *Norfolk Chronicle & Norwich Gazette*, published on Fridays, Norfolk Chronicle Co. Ltd, Market Place
- *Norfolk News*, published on Saturdays, Norfolk News Company, Nos 5–7 Exchange Street

- *Norfolk Daily Standard*, Philip Soman & Son, publishers, London Street
- *Norfolk Weekly Standard & Argus*, Philip Soman & Son, publishers, London Street
- *Norwich Mercury*, published on Tuesdays and Fridays, Norwich Mercury Co., publishers, No. 45 London Street
- *People's Weekly Journal*, Norwich Mercury Co., publishers, No. 45 London Street

SOME UNUSUAL TRADES OF NORWICH IN THE NINETEENTH CENTURY

David Allison, **Truss Maker**, St Peter's Steps
Hannah Amos, **Havel Maker**, Alms Lane
Charles Barnard, **Mangle Maker**, Upper Market
Robert Blake, **Soap Boiler**, St Martin's at Palace Plain
James Blazeby, **Animal Portrait Painter**, Bethel Street
William Dunn, **Lucifer Match Maker**, Silver Road

William Hewett, **Slaie Maker**, Unicorn Yard
William Humfriss, **Cow Keeper**, St Martin's at Oak
John Jaggers, **Treacle Manufacturer**, St Augustine's Gates
Mrs Mary Kitton, **Cardboard Pill Box Maker**, Bull Close
Samuel Knights, **Pattern and Clog Maker**, St Andrew's Hill
Robert Leeds, **Blacking Manufacturer**, Lower Westwick Street
Robert Pinick, **Lime Burner**, Dereham Road
William Pratt, **Fish Manure Manufacturer**, Fish Market
Mrs Ann Robinson, **Cork Cutter**, Bridge Street
William Taney, **Coach and Livery Lace and Fringe Manufacturers**,
    Timberhill
Nathaniel Wyeth, **Brick Burner**, Lakenham

NORWICH BOOT AND SHOE TRADE

As the cloth manufacturing industry declined in Norwich during the nineteenth century, boot and shoe manufacture ascended as one of the major employers. Increasing competition from American imports in the latter half of the nineteenth century saw the greater part of the shoe manufacturing industry invest heavily in the construction of imposing and impressive 'super factories' in order to compete. This investment was often made possible by the amalgamation of larger more successful firms and resulted in companies such as Sexton, Son & Everard or Howlett & White.

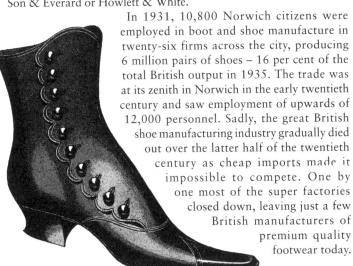

In 1931, 10,800 Norwich citizens were employed in boot and shoe manufacture in twenty-six firms across the city, producing 6 million pairs of shoes – 16 per cent of the total British output in 1935. The trade was at its zenith in Norwich in the early twentieth century and saw employment of upwards of 12,000 personnel. Sadly, the great British shoe manufacturing industry gradually died out over the latter half of the twentieth century as cheap imports made it impossible to compete. One by one most of the super factories closed down, leaving just a few British manufacturers of premium quality footwear today.

HMSO AND ANGLIA SQUARE

Her Majesty's Stationery Office (HMSO) began its move from London to Norwich in early 1967. It took four years of negotiation and planning before the new office block – the award-winning Sovereign House – went up in Anglia Square as part of a £3 million complex which included shops, the new Odeon cinema and a car park for 1,000 vehicles, all designed by Alan Cooke Associates. The Central Computer and Telecommunications Agency (CCTA) took over another building attached to Anglia Square as a satellite office to house part of its procurement wing. HMSO brought about 650 staff up from London and other offices, and made 350 jobs available for local people. Sovereign House suffered a number of critical design flaws and, after twenty-five years, it became too expensive to maintain. Declared no longer fit for purpose, and following the privatisation of HMSO operations, the office moved to St Crispin's House. Today, the modernist Sovereign House building faces demolition in a move to redevelop Anglia Square.

THE PRINCIPLE EMPLOYERS AND EMPLOYEES IN NORWICH IN 1971

Employer	Employees
Laurence, Scott & Electromotors	3,000
Norwich Union	2,600
Rowntree Mackintosh	2,000
Reckitt & Colman	1,500
Norvic Shoes	1,500
Boulton & Paul	1,450
Jarrold & Sons	1,450
Mann Egerton	1,070
HMSO	1,000
R.G. Carter Builders	1,000
Bally Shoes	900
Diamond H. Control	850

A RANGE OF TRADES THROUGH THE YEARS

The earliest known reference to a barber in England was John Belton, a Norwich barber recorded as resident in the city in 1163.

Norwich had a huge livestock market from the thirteenth century that, by the nineteenth century, spread across 8.5 acres, stretching from the Castle Ditches, across the Cattle Market in front of the castle and around to beside Agricultural Hall Plain. In the 1930s, it was one of the largest cattle markets in the country. Six firms of auctioneers and thirty-three private dealers sold 212,000 head of livestock per annum – representing a cash value on initial sales of £1,250,000. Fowl and turkey sales were also successful and exceeded 100,000 head per annum.

Dragon Hall, situated on the ancient King Street in Norwich, is the only known surviving medieval merchant's trading hall in Western Europe. It was built by Robert Toppes (1404–67) to display his wares.

Anthony de Solempne, originally from Brabant in the southern Netherlands and part of the Stranger community of Dutch refugees, was the first Norwich printer. He arrived in 1567 and established his business at the sign of the White Dove before moving to the Edinburgh Arms on Dove Street.

England's first provincial newspaper *The Norwich Post* was printed in the city by Francis Burges. The first edition appeared on 6 September 1701.

William Stark was an able Norwich chemist in the early nineteenth century, and one of the first dyers of fabrics of Norwich manufacture, particularly of the colour turkey red.

Matthew Joy, 'The Walking Baker', died in June 1823. For the last eleven years of his life, Joy had carried his large basket of bread (weighing around 8 stone) on his shoulders to make his deliveries to outlying villages around Norwich, a journey of about 20 miles a day. It was calculated that over that time he had walked around 68,440 miles.

The first person in Norwich to advertise patent photographic portraits was Mr Beard of the Royal Bazaar who promoted his trade in December 1843, with prices ranging from 1 to 2 guineas. These likenesses were stated to be 'surprisingly correct', and severe chemical tests 'proved that they would last to infinity'.

Thomas Edward Gunn (1844–1923) was a respected taxidermist who specialised in birds. Based in Gunn Court, Upper St Giles Street, he was awarded medals and honours for his skill in this craft and the business of T.E. Gunn of Norwich became the largest taxidermists in the city with a reputation that spread across the country. Gunn's son Frederick followed his father into the business; retiring in 1941, aged 72. The firm finally closed its doors in 1950, after almost 100 years of continuous trading.

In the mid-nineteenth century, mulberry trees were planted in the city with the aim of introducing the growth of silk to the trade of the city (silk moths only feed on mulberry trees).

George Allen of St Stephen's was the first to introduce the manufacture of elastic cloth to Norwich in November 1860.

The first screw steamboat built in Norwich was launched from Field's boatbuilding yard at Carrow Abbey, on 10 March 1868. She was named *Alexandra* and was intended for passenger traffic on the local rivers. The proud owner of the vessel was Mr John Hart Boughen.

The Norwich Co-operative Society, with its head office at No. 58 St Stephen's Street, was truly a city institution. It started operations in the city in 1875 with 119 members, £135 of share capital and sales amounting to £493. Sixty years later, in 1935, the membership was 25,036, sales amounted to £650,000 and there was an annual distribution of dividend amounting to £50,000.

When William Cooke Stafford died in Norwich in December 1877, aged 83, he was one of the oldest working journalists in the country.

In the 1890s, the Great Eastern Railway cattle station at Trowse had thirteen lairs and nineteen loading pens on the departure side of the line, capable of storing 2,000 head of cattle and 4,000 sheep. On the other side were nine lairs and thirteen pens that could store 1,500 cattle and 3,000 sheep. The lairs and pens covered a total of nearly 7 acres.

In early March 1912, the Board of Trade appointed the first female supervising officers to the women's department of Labour Exchanges to encourage women to work and to canvass employers. The woman appointed for Norwich was Miss E.E. Page. She certainly had a task on her hands though, as her official area was entitled 'East Midlands' and embraced a large chunk of eastern England, from Nottingham to Ipswich.

Boulton & Paul developed and built the Boulton Bodmin for the Air Ministry at Norwich in 1923, the first British all-metal bomber.

During the 1930s, Herbert Rumsey Wells created and manufactured the 'Doggie' cap at his premises on St Andrew's Street. He proudly claimed to be 'the most expensive cap maker in the world' and the caps could be cut and assembled to special order within four hours. In 1938, prices started at 15*s* 6*d* and went up to a massive 42*s* each.

Norwich shoemakers Norvic exported nearly 210,000 pairs of shoes to Russia in 1970.

7

THAT'S ENTERTAINMENT

STAR TURNS

The medieval Wayland Wood near Watton is said to be the setting for the story *Babes in the Wood* and the first known publication of the tale was in Norwich in 1595. The Theatre Royal often performed pantomimes 'founded on [this] celebrated and world known Norfolk Ballad', including *The Babes in the Wood, and Harlequin and the Cruel Uncle, or the Forest Queen of the Fairy Dell* shown in December 1859. In 1874, Mr F. Robson offered *The Babes in the Wood, or Harlequin Robin Hood and the Fairies of the Forest*, produced at Norwich Theatre by Mr Richard Younge's company.

Comic actor and dancer Will Kempe danced the Morris from the Mansion House, London to the churchyard of St Peter Mancroft, Norwich. He called the journey his 'Nine Days Wonder' and travelled on nine days spread out over four weeks during February and March 1599.

Pablo Fanque (born William Derby), the first black circus proprietor in Britain, was born in Norwich in 1796. Some of the entertainers 'late of Pablo Fanque's Fair' are mentioned in The Beatles song on 'Being For the Benefit of Mr Kite' on their *Sergeant Pepper* album after Lennon was inspired by an old billposter advertisement for their show.

Entertainer Ching Lao Lauro of Drury Lane received what was described as 'the worst review in the history of performance in Norwich' in April 1828. The newspaper critic did not mince his words after watching the enactment of *The Man in the Moon*: 'No viler tissue of nonsensical stuff could be foisted on the patience of an insulted audience. It had more revolting coarseness and infinitely less ingenuity than ever characterised the worst puppet shows' clumsiest performers.' Lauro fared no better with his second act of *Harlequin in the Shades* for it, 'Descended to the lowest vault of the Capulets, amidst universal hisses which such execrable trash duly called forth.'

The greatest violinist of his day, Niccolò Paganini performed at the Corn Exchange, Norwich on 28 and 29 July 1829 and at the theatre on 30 July. He was curiously described in the local press as a 'fascinating, but by no means fair-dealing, foreigner'.

The Norfolk and Norwich Horticultural Society staged the first Chrysanthemum Show held in Britain in 1829.

Virtuoso pianist and composer Franz Lizst played concerts at the Assembly Rooms and theatre in Norwich in September 1840.

On 12 April 1851, Mr Fred Phillips was performing the part of Rob Roy at Norwich Theatre when he fell from a 'fictitious precipice' and greatly injured his lower leg. Surgeons at the Norfolk and Norwich Hospital deemed it necessary to amputate this section of the leg and it was noted that Phillips underwent the operation with 'heroic fortitude'.

Miss Tubby was a box-keeper at Norwich Theatre for many years and was highly respected for her remarkable fund of information about local theatrical matters. For nearly half a century, 'Miss Tubby's Night' was one of the principal events in the Norwich season. She died at Doughty's Hospital on 25 June 1853.

An alarming accident occurred in a building erected for equestrian performances at the Orchard Gardens, Norwich, on 30 November 1857. Soon after the commencement of the entertainment, the supports of the gallery gave way, and the structure fell, with between 300 and 400 people in it. The whole mass of timber collapsed under the people, who, along with their seats, were thrown outwards, rolling over one another. By some miracle nobody was killed, no legs or arms broken, and nobody was seriously hurt.

Mr Phineas T. Barnum, the celebrated showman, lectured at St Andrew's Hall on 14 February 1859 on the subject of 'Money-making and the Art of Humbug'. The lecture was described as 'a strange medley – a most anomalous production'.

The celebrated dwarf, 'General' Tom Thumb (real name Charles Sherwood Stratton), held a series of levees at St Andrew's Hall in April 1859. He travelled from the hall in his miniature carriage, drawn by the smallest ponies in the world and attended by an African coachman and footman in livery.

On 11 October 1859, Charles Dickens gave a reading of *A Christmas Carol* and the trial scene from *The Pickwick Papers* at St Andrew's Hall. The following night he read the story of Little Dombey and of Mrs Gamp. It was commented, 'His voice was far from powerful but he had remarkable expression and the power of exhibiting this in face as well as in voice.'

The celebrated tight-rope walker, Blondin, made his first appearance to the Norwich people on 2 August 1861. The rope was fixed at an altitude of about 60ft, in a field on Newmarket Road. It was commented, however, that: 'It is a very fortunate circumstance for M. Blondin that he crossed Niagara and had the Prince of Wales for a spectator, for it has added a much greater interest to his performances than they would otherwise have acquired, and even, if we may judge from what we saw here, they deserved.'

Professor J.H. Pepper lectured at Noverre's Rooms, Norwich, on the subject of optical illusions, and for the first time, exhibited in the city the now well-known illusion 'Pepper's Ghost' on 16 March 1863.

Chang, the Chinese giant, was exhibited at the Lecture Hall, St Andrew's in August 1868. He was described as 'between 8½ft and 9ft high, and his natural suavity of manner is very agreeable to those he meets'.

Captain Bates, the 'Kentucky Giant' (real name Martin Van Buren Bates) stood 7ft 9in (2.36m) tall and weighed 470lb). Along with the American conjoined twins, Chrissie and Millie McKoy (better known as the 'Two-headed Nightingale'), he appeared in St Andrew's on 21 May 1870. Of the girls it was said, 'Chrissie and Millie are fairly educated, and sing either solos or duets with ease and effect'.

The first 'spelling bee' to test the orthographical and philological knowledge of the competitors in Norwich was held at Noverre's Rooms, Norwich, on 19 January 1876. The mayor, Mr J.H. Tillett, presided, Mr T. Richmond Pinder was interrogator, referees were Mr Carlos Cooper, the Revd A.C. Copeman and Mr A. Master, and their decisions were in accordance with the Imperial, Richardson's, and Walker's dictionaries.

Oscar Wilde lectured before a large audience in the Assembly Room of the Agricultural Hall on the subject of 'The House Beautiful' and decorative art on 20 March 1884.

The phonograph described as 'Edison's wonderful talking machine' was exhibited for the first time in Norwich by Mr William Lynd on 26 April 1889.

Jerome K. Jerome, the author of *Three Men in a Boat* and *Idle Thoughts of an Idle Fellow*, gave a lecture at the Assembly Room of the Agricultural Hall on 'Humour, Old and New' on 3 October 1894.

Louis Tussaud's 'All the World in Wax' exhibition was opened at the Agricultural Hall on 25 May 1896. One of the attractions was the display, for the first time in Norwich, of cinematography or 'living pictures'.

Barnum & Bailey's 'Greatest Show on Earth' came to Norwich in September 1898. Located on a piece of land on Unthank Road, more than 42,000 people visited the show over two days.

Sir Edward Elgar and Sir Henry Wood were the conductors for 'The Kingdom' and 'Hymn of Praise', respectively, at the Norfolk and Norwich Triennial Musical Festival on Friday, 27 October 1911.

Founded by and very much the vision of Nugent Monck, the Maddermarket Theatre – opened in 1921 – was the first permanent recreation of an Elizabethan Theatre in Britain. George Bernard Shaw wrote to Monck in 1940: 'There is nothing in British theatrical history more extraordinary than your creation of the Maddermarket Theatre ...'

In November 1923, Boyah, a 7-year-old elephant from the Royal Italian Circus that was appearing at the Hippodrome, broke down a wall dividing his stall from warehouse wholesale fruiterer Mr H.C. Stanton of Bethel Street and ate a large grass basket, 4 stones of English onions, Brazil nuts and other fruits and vegetables.

Comedy duo Stan Laurel and Oliver Hardy performed at the Norwich Hippodrome in February 1954.

The Beatles performed only once in Norwich, at the Grosvenor Rooms on Prince of Wales Road on 17 May 1963. The fab four were supported by Ricky Lee and the Hucklebucks. Some 1,700 people squeezed into the former ballroom, despite the price being upped from the usual 2s 6d for a Friday night, to 7s 6d!

Legendary rock guitarist Jimi Hendrix played at the Orford Cellar at Norwich on 25 January 1967.

THE THEATRE ROYAL

The first theatre in Norwich was established when the White Swan Inn became the resident home of the Norwich Company of Comedians in 1731, the following year it became known as the White Swan Playhouse. The first purpose-built theatre was constructed by Thomas Ivory in 1757 and opened as the New Theatre on 31 January 1758. An Act of Parliament for licensing the theatre received royal assent in 1768 and it became known as the Theatre Royal thereafter. In 1826, William Wilkins built the second Theatre Royal a short distance away, on the site still occupied by the current venue. The theatre was gutted by fire on 22 June 1934. Built anew, the Theatre Royal reopened on 30 September 1935 and, despite threats to its future and even a closure in 1990, it has been extensively refurbished and extended, and continues to go from strength to strength.

GUILD DAY

Celebrated for the last time on 16 June 1835, Guild Day was once one of the greatest annual occasions in the city. The Tuesday before the eve of John the Baptist's Day was the day of the inauguration of the mayor-elect and there would be a cavalcade that could almost rival London's Lord Mayor's procession. First in place was a large green and gold dragon, affectionately known to the citizens as 'Snap' – usually a skilfully painted canvas-covered wooden framework worn by a performer. 'Snap' was remembered as a remarkably civil and witty dragon, full of cunning tricks and wise sayings. He had four 'whifflers' with drawn swords to wait on him and clear the way for the rest of the procession. This they did by brandishing their short swords with the greatest dexterity and making a ready way through any crowd without hurting anyone; although any boy wishing to cheekily linger too long could receive a deft slap on the legs with the flat of the sword. After 'Snap' and the 'whifflers' came the mayor, aldermen and important personages mounted on horseback with music, flags and paraphernalia. In this way they made their way to the cathedral, which on the occasion was always strewed with rushes. 'Snap' would wait outside (he was a creature of the Devil after all) but the rest of the procession would enter the cathedral for a sermon. After the sermon they would repair to the hall, where dinner would be provided for 800 or 900 persons (including ladies among the diners).

The final Guild Day, in 1835, included a civic procession to the cathedral. 'Snap', too, made his final appearance. Chambers, the senior boy at the Free Grammar School, under the Revd Henry Banfather, delivered the Latin oration and was presented with five guineas' worth of books by Mr Moore the mayor-elect, who made a similar present to Norgate, the orator on the preceding Guild Day. In the course of the proceedings at the Guildhall, it was decided to petition the House of Lords against the Bill to provide for the regulation of Municipal Corporations in England and Wales. Some 800 guests attended the Guild feast at St Andrew's Hall, and a ball was given at the Assembly Rooms in the evening.

THINGS AIN'T WHAT THEY USED TO BE

When the Norwich Waterworks were opened in September 1851, the event was publicly celebrated. The band of the Coldstream Guards played selections in the Market Place, 220 guests dined at the Assembly Rooms under the presidency of Mr Samuel Bignold, chairman of the Waterworks Company, and 20,000 persons witnessed a display of fireworks in the Market Place.

NOT TO BE MISSED!

The title of the 1855 Christmas pantomime produced at the Theatre Royal was *King Goggle-eyed Greedy Gobble and the Fairy of the Enchanted Lake*. Or perhaps the offering of *The Sleeping Beauty in the Wood, or Harlequin and the Spiteful Ogress and the Seven Fairy Godmothers from the Realm of Golden Flowers* from 1858 is appealing? The year 1864 would see *Snowdrop, King Bonbon, and the Seven Elves, or the Magic Mirror and the Fatal Sewing Machine*. The mind boggles.

PLAYING 'THE FIELD' – VICTORIAN STYLE

High summer in Norwich in the mid-1890s saw many young men and ladies congregate in Chapel Field Gardens ready for the start of the band concerts at 7 p.m. Entrance was charged at 3*d* but on special illuminated nights – when Chinese lanterns were draped over the trees and fairy lamps lay along the borders – it was 6*d*. There were no electric lights – a man had to go around at dusk with a taper to light each one, which contained a nightlight, and the ambience was the height of romance in its day.

By 8.30 the grounds would be swelled with city folk and the young men, usually in pairs, would cast a roving eye at the young ladies as they sauntered by, also in pairs, wearing enormous straw hats piled high with flowers. A favourite haunt was under a great chestnut tree with hard metal seats that ringed around its trunk. Here couples would remain aloof until the bolder of the men plucked up enough courage to make some remark and break the ice.

THE HIPPODROME

The Hippodrome began life in 1903 as the Grand Opera House, with a magnificent frontage designed by London architect W.G.R. Sprague and seating inside for 2,000 people. Responding to the demand for more popular entertainment, the theatre was renamed the Hippodrome and it became one of Norfolk's premier music halls. Over the years many stars appeared there, including Max Miller, Laurel and Hardy, Tommy Trinder and Jack Storey. David Lloyd George spoke there and a 12-year-old acrobat named Archie Leach made his stage debut there in 1916 – he became better known as the suave Hollywood actor Cary Grant. Sadly times changed, television took away a lot of the regulars and, unable to continue, the Hippodrome closed for the last time in 1960 and was demolished in 1966 to make way for a multi-storey car park.

KISSING IN NORWICH

An unusual novelty postcard from about 1905 explains the following:

I have just finished a tour around town and have come to the conclusion that Norwich Girls make kissing a fine art. This is my experience:

St Augustine Girls close their eyes and dreamily suggest some
more secluded spot.

Carrow Girls cling very tightly and keep murmuring
'Just once more'.

Catton Girls try to look very stern, squeeze your hand
and afterwards tell you that 'You ought to be ashamed
of yourself'.

Mousehold Girls make a meal of it and murmur,
'Nothing shall come between us'.

Thorpe Girls throw their arms around your neck and tell you
'The more you do it, the better they love you'.

Trowse Girls become very excited, try to bite your ear and
leave you an absolute wreck.

A NIGHT AT THE FLICKS

Norwich cinemas extant in 1955:

The Capitol, Aylsham Road
The Carlton, All Saints Green
The Gaumont, Haymarket
The Mayfair, Magdalen Street
The Norvic, Prince of Wales Road
The Noverre, Theatre Street
The Odeon, Botolph Street
The Regal, Dereham Road
The Regent, Prince of Wales Road
The Ritz, Dereham Road
The Theatre de Luxe, St Andrew Street

ANGLIA TV TREATS

Anglia Television first went on air on 27 October 1959. The Anglia
Television rotating silver knight was used as its logo from 1959
to 1988 and the musical fanfare which accompanied each of its
appearances was a snatch of Handel's *Water Music* specially arranged
by Sir Malcolm Sargent.

'And now, from Norwich, it's the quiz of the week!' was the
catchphrase of Nicolas Parsons who presented 'Sale of the Century',
which ran between 1971–83. The iconic theme tune 'Joyful Pete'

(so named in a gesture to the director, Peter Joy) was composed by Peter Fenn, director of music at Anglia, who played live on his organ at every recording.

Gambit, based on the card game pontoon, was another winning Anglia quiz show. Hosted by Fred Dinage (1975–82) and Tom O'Connor (1983–85), it featuring Miss Anglia finalist Michelle Lambourne as hostess on almost every episode.

Bygones, the documentary series that explored East Anglian history and traditional crafts, ran from 1967 until 1989. For most of those years the show was presented by the affectionately remembered Dick Joice, until his retirement in 1987 when film historian John Huntley took over.

Sir David Frost, master of satire and responsible for some of the most important political interviews of the twentieth century, made his first screen appearance on Anglia Television's *Town And Gown* series.

The famous drawing room introduction scene for each of the *Roald Dahl's Tales of the Unexpected* was actually filmed on a specially designed set in a studio at Anglia House.

No Sunday lunchtime was complete back in the 1970s without *Farming Diary* and its distinctive title sequence tune 'Blow Away the Morning Dew' from Ralph Vaughn Williams' *English Folk Song Suite*.

The CITV series *Knightmare*, which has now garnered a cult status, was filmed at Anglia TV studios. *Knightmare* ran for eight series between 1987 and 1994, and at its peak attracted a massive 4–5 million viewers per episode.

SOME FILMS AND TV PROGRAMMES MADE IN OR FEATURING NORWICH

Norwich Air Pageant (1927), a newsreel story made by the Topical Film Company.

The newsreel film *The Gate to the Broads – Norwich* (1934) was made by British Pathé and takes a charming look at the popular features of the city.

A Fine City Norwich (1953), a documentary showing the historical and industrial aspects of the city, was made for Norwich Union.

Come With Me to Norwich (1953), a Richard Dimbleby travelogue.

The Story of Magdalen Street (1960), a film sponsored by the Civic Trust to record the redevelopment of Magdalen Street.

The arts series *Omnibus* filmed part of their episode *Van Gogh* (1990) in Norwich.

BBC Look East has been broadcast from Norwich since it was first aired on 5 October 1959.

You Can Enjoy Life at the Norwich Union (1967), showing a variety of jobs in the offices, was made for Norwich Union.

The Go Between (1970), starring Julie Christie and Alan Bates, had filming centred around Melton Constable Hall but used many other locations in the county, including Tombland in Norwich.

Monty Python's *And Now for Something Completely Different* (1971) had scenes shot near Norwich Castle and Elm Hill.

Norwich Renewal (1974), a documentary made by the Central Office of Information.

Our Miss Fred (1974), starring Danny la Rue, had scenes shot on Elm Hill, Norwich, and other locations in the county.

Norwich (1976), a TV documentary made by Thames TV featuring John Julius Norwich.

Memoirs of a Survivor (1981), starring Julie Christie and Nigel Hawthorne, was filmed on Argyle Street.

Tales of the Unexpected, now revered as a cult series, was produced by Anglia TV (1979–88) and used many locations around the county. In Norwich, locations included Norwich Union's Marble Hall ('Completely Foolproof'), Elm Hill ('Stranger in Town'), Windsor Bishop jewellers on London Street ('The Evesdropper') and in other episodes Upper St Giles, Princes Street and Bowthorpe cemetery in Norwich all make an appearance.

The Channel 4 show *Treasure Hunt*, where Anneka Rice was directed to collect clues by contestants in the studio armed with maps and reference books, saw her come to Norwich and Norfolk in 1985.

Lovejoy (1986–94), starring Ian McShane, was mostly filmed in Suffolk but the series included a few locations in Norwich, notably Elm Hill.

Although the film *Clockwise* (1986) has star John Cleese doing all he can to make it on time to an important conference at the University of Norwich, none of it is actually filmed in Norwich or Norfolk.

Wilt (1990), starring Griff Rhys Jones, Alison Steadman and Mel Smith, had a number of scenes shot around Norwich, including Rose Lane car park (now demolished), St Giles Street, St George's, St Augustine's Street and Guildhall Hill.

Anglia TV drama series *The Chief* (1990–95) was filmed across East Anglia, with Tim Piggott-Smith and then Martin Shaw in the lead role. Norwich locations were regularly used, including the now demolished Boulton & Paul Works on Riverside and the Old Brewery Store, Mountergate as police offices, Pigg Lane became a red light area and the Rhône-Poulenc site was, well … a factory site. They even used special effects to blow up the Royal Arcade!

The *Kavanagh QC* episode 'Innocency of Life' (1995), starring John Thaw, included scenes filmed in Norwich Cathedral, the cathedral cloisters and The Close.

Stardust (2007), starring Robert de Niro and Michelle Pfeiffer, saw major conversion of Elm Hill to a fantasy Middles Ages-style street.

The popular BBC *Who Do You Think You Are?* programme was filmed around the city, notably on Ber Street and Elm Hill, when cookery legend Mary Berry looked at the story of her Norwich ancestors (aided by local historian Neil Storey) in 2014.

Scenes for *Avengers: Age of Ultron* (2015), starring Robert Downey Junior, were filmed around the Sainsbury Centre for Visual Arts on the UEA campus.

The fictional biography of Alan Partridge (the comedy TV character played by Steve Coogan) tells how Alan grew up in Norwich and became a broadcaster on the fictional Radio Norwich after the decline of his TV career as a sports commentator and chat show host. Scenes of Alan in and around Norwich often feature in episodes of the various Partridge series. The feature film *Alpha Papa* (2013) also featured scenes shot around the city.

WHERE WE USED TO PLAY

Parks and playgrounds extant in Norwich in 1942:

Chapel Field Gardens and Playground (8.5 acres), Chapel Field Road
Eagle Baths Playground (1 acre), Heigham Street
Earlham Park (160 acres), Earlham Road
Eaton Park (80 acres), South Park Avenue
Gildencroft Recreation Ground (2 acres), St Augustine's
Heigham Park (6 acres), Recreation Road
Hellesdon Mill Meadow, Hellesdon Low Road
Hellesdon Recreation Ground (29 acres), Hellesdon
Jenny Lind Playground (1 rod 13 poles), Pottergate
Jubilee Playground (8 acres), Long John's Hill, Lakenham
Kett's Cave (3.5 acres), Morley Street, Mousehold Street
King Street Playground (1 rod 20 poles), King Street
Lakenham Baths Recreation Ground (1.5 acres), Martineau Lane
Lakenham Recreation Ground (1.5 acres), City Road, Lakenham

Mile Cross Gardens (1.5 acres), Aylsham Road
Mousehold Heath (190 acres), Mousehold
Mousehold Woodland Estate (31 acres), Mousehold
Priory Playground (1 rod 24 poles), Cowgate
St James' Hollow (6 acres), Gurney Road, Mousehold
Sewell Park (3 acres), Constitution Hill, New Catton
The James Stuart Gardens (0.5 acre), Recorder Road
Waterloo Park (17 acres), Angel Road
Wensum Park (8 acres), Drayton Road
Wensum View Recreation Ground (1 acre), Dereham Road
Woodlands Plantation (6.5 acres), Dereham Road
Woodrow Pilling Park (7.5 acres), Harvey Lane, Thorpe

RADIO TIMES

On 20 June 1961, Radio Norwich became the BBC's first local broadcasting experiment in their 'Midland Region'. The radio show came into being at 6.28 a.m., included features on fashion and letters from Norwich people and there was even a live broadcast via a radio car from a local market. Radio Norwich continued until 7.32 p.m. when it closed down with local news headlines. In the analysis of the broadcast, concern was expressed that the interviews were not lively enough and that 'perhaps it would be difficult if not impossible to find sufficient material to keep going'. It was also commented that 'An obvious fault, considering that much of the service will be a background to the housewife's daily chores, was the length of interviews with citizens of Norwich. Some of which extended to five minutes or more with one person.'

Radio Norfolk was the first BBC Local Radio station for the region on 11 September 1980. It was based in a former carpet showroom at Norfolk Tower on Surrey Street until their move to The Forum in 2003. BBC Radio Norfolk has frequently gained some of the highest audience figures of any of the BBC's local radio stations in England.

Radio Broadland first aired on 1 October 1984. The main base for the station was on St George's Plain, Colegate, and popular Broadland presenters included Nick Risby, Tony Gilham, Dave Brown, Rob Chandler and Chrissy Jackson. Even 'Whispering Bob' Harris presented a weekly show for a while when he was living in the area. In January 2009, Radio Broadland was renamed Heart Norwich

as part of a major rebranding of twenty-nine stations owned by Global Radio.

Future Radio, a community-based radio station for and by the people of Norwich, ran its first restricted service license for Norwich from 3–29 May 2004.

Some of the affectionately remembered voices of Radio Norfolk are no longer with us, including Don Shepherd and his *Dad's Favourite Tunes* show; consumer champion John Mills, who presented his *Midday with Mills* programme until his death after a long battle with cancer in March 2006; and John Taylor MBE, who presented and produced *John Taylor's Radio Times* for twenty years until his death, aged 85, in November 2006. At the time of his passing he was believed to be the country's oldest radio presenter and producer. And who could forget Roy Waller, afternoon broadcasting legend, *Rodeo Norfolk* country music programme presenter and unbiased Norwich City football match commentator who died in July 2010 aged 69.

Another station, 99.9 Radio Norwich, 'The New Number of Norwich', opened on 29 June 2006. Programmes were kicked off by Tom Kay at 8.30 a.m. with the 1979 single 'Good Times' by Chic.

BOOKWORM WITH A CONSCIENCE

We all enjoy a good book but some people take it to an extreme. In December 1962, a man contacted a member of library staff concerned that he had some overdue books. He was assured that if he returned them no questions would be asked. He pulled up at the library in a van and unloaded 299 books which had been taken out illegally; some of which had been listed as missing by the library as early as 1946. City Librarian Philip Hepworth commented that the staff were 'flabbergasted' but he assured the man that as far as the library was concerned the matter was closed.

8

SPORTING TIMES

NORWICH, A CITY OF SPORT

Cricket bat makers require wide-ringed timber, free of knots and of a uniform light colour, the best being *Salix alba* var. *Caerulea* was first discovered by John Crowe and grown in his salicetum at Norwich in the eighteenth century.

Three gentlemen, for a considerable wager, undertook to walk blindfolded from Post Office Court to the great doors of St Peter Mancroft church in fifteen minutes on 18 October 1802. Two of them performed this task in less than the given time, much to the satisfaction of the spectators, but the other unfortunate gentleman bent his course rapidly for the Upper Market, and found himself at the expiration of the time at the great doors of St Andrew's Hall.

Public cockfights were still being held on the bowling green at Chapel Field in the early nineteenth century. Cockfighting was only banned outright in England and Wales in 1835.

On 9 June 1853, a cricket match between eighteen of Norwich and eleven of All England commenced on the new Cricket Ground on Newmarket Road. Concluding on the 11th, the score was Norwich, 110–46; All England, 58–70.

Foot-racing was revived by Mr Thomas Sapey, a local sportsman, on the Old Cricket Ground at a meeting staged over 3–4 July 1854. A 1-mile handicap, open to all England, brought twenty-four competitors, among whom were Thomas Horspool of Sheffield (holder of the 1-mile champion belt), Mr C. Welton of Gateshead, William Newman of London, Robert Bunn, John 'The Milk Boy' of Brighton, Richard Fromow, William 'Cock' Blyth and the well-known local pugilist Jem Mace.

Celebrated pedestrian Robert Bunn ran a mile against time on the Ipswich Road, Norwich for a wager of £25 on 6 August 1857. The wager was that he would not cover the distance in four minutes forty-five seconds. He accomplished the feat in four minutes thirty seconds.

An extraordinary leap was made by a horse ridden by Mr William Feek, horse trainer, of Norwich in August 1857. In the presence of a number of gentlemen, Feek displayed the power of the animal by jumping it over a high fence on Newmarket Road. The horse made the jump without touching it, completing a spring which, from point to point, was 34ft.

The first annual dinner of the Norfolk and Norwich Anglers' Society was held on 30 March 1858 at the Bell Hotel, Norwich, under the presidency of Mr R.N. Bacon.

On 18 August 1859, the first recorded angling match in Norfolk took place at Limpenhoe Reach, on the Yare, for prizes given by Mr C.J. Greene of Rose Lane, Norwich. The total weight of fish taken by the twenty-eight competitors in the course of eight hours was 16st 7lbs 1oz. Mr G. Harman secured first prize, with a catch of 33lbs 3ozs.

In June 1861, celebrated chessplayer Herr Kolisch contested thirteen games simultaneously against some of the best players in the neighbourhood at the Rampant Horse Hotel, Norwich. He won eight games, lost three, and two were drawn.

On 30 October 1862, a 10-mile race, for a silver cup of the value of £30, took place between the Indian Deerfoot and Brighten, 'The Norwich Milk Boy', on Figg's Cricket Ground, Newmarket Road, Norwich. Previous performances of Brighten and Deerfoot had given rise to suspicions as to the genuineness of these contests, but on this occasion it was announced that, as Deerfoot's career in England was about to terminate, the race would be a legitimate trial of speed. Brighten won by 30yds, in fifty-four minutes, thirty seconds.

The Norfolk and Norwich Gymnastic Society held their first annual sports event on the Newmarket Road Cricket Ground in May 1866. The programme included gymnastic exercises, boxing, high jumping, and flat or hurdle racing.

The first annual regatta of the Norfolk and Norwich Rowing Club was held at Whitlingham on 16 September 1867.

A skating rink, built at the cost of £9,000, was opened at St Giles Street on 19 September 1876. Sadly its popularity was short lived for on 26 May 1877 it was announced: 'The passion for rinking having fallen to zero, the managers have introduced additional attractions in the shape of a couple of clever bicyclists and a troupe of performing dogs.' A theatrical licence was subsequently obtained and the rink was opened as the Vaudeville Theatre of Varieties on 10 September 1877.

The first annual meeting of the Norfolk and Norwich Bicycle Club was held at the Grapes Hotel on 1 January 1877 and the first road race took place on 30 April. Six competitors entered the race, which ran from the Grapes Hotel on Unthank Road to Wymondham, Wicklewood and thence to Carleton Forehoe, through Colney and Earlham, to the top of Belvoir Street, Earlham Road; a distance of about 24 miles. The winner was Mr J. Campling. The club uniform consisted of a cloth helmet with a metallic monogram in front, a smart dark grey tunic, and knickerbockers.

The Norwich Amateur Bicycle Club was formed in 1879. Active cycling groups in the city also included the East Anglian Cycling Club (founded 1921), Cyclists' Touring Club, Norfolk District Association, and the Norco Wheelers Cycling Club.

WILLMOTTS 1910—1948

38 YEARS
ESTABLISHED
–AND STILL AT
YOUR SERVICE

"*It's time you had a BSA*"

TENNIS AND ALL SPORTS EQUIPMENT
•
CYCLES AUTOCYCLES AND MOTOR CYCLES
•
REPAIRS AND ACCESSORIES

"Travelling to Eaton Park fo Tennis is so much easier when you've a B.S.A. You don't have to wait about for buses—and the fare money you save soon pays for one of these magnificent machines. Come along today—and chose *your* B.S.A."

Officially appointed dealers for :—

B.S.A. and SUNBEAM
CYCLES & SERVICE
Generous pay - as - you - ride terms

WRITE OR VISIT      TELEPHONE 23101

—WILLBRO HOUSE—
43-51 PRINCE OF WALES RD. NORWICH

OPEN ALL DAY — EVERY SHOPPING DAY

The twelve hours' roller skating championship of the Eastern Counties was competed for at St Giles Hall, on 6 March 1879. The winner was Candler of Norwich, who covered 77 miles 7 laps between 8 a.m. and 8 p.m.

The Royal Norwich Golf Club was formed in 1893.

Professional golfer Arthur Gladstone Havers (1898–1980) was born in Norwich. Havers first qualified for the Open in 1914 when he was just 16 years old and went on to win the Open Championship at Royal Troon in 1923. He also played in the Ryder Cup in 1927, 1931 and 1933.

Norwich-born Humphrey Colman Boardman (1904–98) competed for Great Britain at the 1928 Summer Olympics in Amsterdam and was a member of the English boat team that won the gold medal in the coxed fours competition as well as in the eights contest at the 1930 Empire Games, the first of what would be later known as the Commonwealth Games.

The first game of baseball on the grounds at Newmarket Road was played on 25 May 1918.

Miss E. Downes of Eaton (Norwich) Rifle Club won the Ladies' Cup at Bisley in July 1924.

Norwich Viking Motorcycle Club was founded in 1927.

The Canadian sport of log rolling was demonstrated in Norwich in 1935.

In the 1950s, Norwich had two tracks for greyhound racing – one at Boundary Park on Boundary Road, Mile Cross and the other at Norwich City Stadium on Sprowston Road.

Darts player Darren 'Demolition Man' Webster was born in Norwich in 1966.

Professional snooker player Barry Pinches was born in Norwich in 1970.

John Hudson, the 25-year-old professional golfer at Hendon, achieved a hole-in-one twice in succession during the second round of the Martini golf tournament at the Royal Norwich Golf Course on 11 June 1971.

NORWICH BOXING

Jem Mace (1831–1910) was the Norfolk pugilist regarded as the 'father' of modern scientific boxing and Champion of England in 1861. Mace went to America in 1868 and toured with the celebrated American boxer John C. Heenan, giving exhibitions of boxing with gloves on. In 1870, Mace defeated Tom Allen at Kenner, Louisiana to become World Boxing Champion. After his return to England, Mace kept the Swan Inn in Norwich for a number of years. He was inducted into the Ring Boxing Hall of Fame in 1954 and the International Boxing Hall of Fame in 1990.

On 19 October 1971, boxing legend, World Heavyweight Champion Muhammad Ali came to the supermarket of T.W. Downs in St Stephen's as part of a promotional tour for Ovaltine.

Former lightweight boxer Jon Thaxton, who held both European and British lightweight boxing titles during his seventeen-year career, was born in Norwich in 1974.

Local boxing legend Arthur 'Ginger' Sadd of Norwich boxed over the years 1929–51. He was a top ten middleweight contender, a world-class fighter who fought over 200 bouts and held both the Eastern Area Welterweight and Middleweight titles. He beat many of the top welter and middleweight contenders of his era, yet only got one shot at a British title when he challenged the redoubtable Jock McAvoy for the British and Empire Middleweight titles in May 1939. Sadd was not a big puncher but he was a master craftsman in the ring. He continued to box when he was well past his prime but his boxing skills were enough for him to hold his own with the best middleweights of the 1940s. A great local character to the end, Sadd passed away on 10 April 1992.

THE MAN WHO BOUGHT WEMBLEY

Arthur Elvin was born in Norwich in 1899. He left school at 14 and, after serving in the Royal Flying Corps during the First World War, was working in a cigarette kiosk at the British Empire Exhibition at Wembley in 1924 when he decided to have a go at running his own shops in the grounds. He bought eight shops for a grand total of £100 and had made over £1,000 profit by the end of the exhibition. At the end of the exhibition an entrepreneur bought the grounds and Elvin became a demolition contractor to clear the site. He bought the buildings one by one and sold off the scrap. Then, when Wembley Stadium went into liquidation, he offered to buy it for £127,000, with a down payment of £12,000. Elvin ended up buying the stadium from its new owners Wembley Company after complications following the death of the original titleholder. They then bought it back from him, leaving Elvin with a very healthy profit. Instead of cash, however, Elvin was given shares, which gave him the largest stake in the stadium and he became chairman. Elvin also created a new indoor multipurpose sports arena alongside the stadium – the Empire Pool and Sports Arena for the 1934 British Empire Games – later renamed Wembley Arena. Elvin was granted a knighthood for his role in staging the 1948 Olympic Games.

NORWICH CITY FOOTBALL CLUB

On the Ball City!

Norwich City Football Club was formed following a meeting at the Criterion Cafe in Norwich on 17 June 1902. The club's song 'On the Ball City' is thought to be the oldest British football chant still being sung today. The song is older than the club itself, having originally been penned for Norwich Teachers or Caley's FC in the 1890s and adapted and adopted by Norwich City in 1902. The club played its first regular matches upon a ground on Newmarket Road, moving to their first purpose-built ground known as the 'The Nest' (constructed on the site of a disused chalk pit on Rosary Road) in 1908. They moved to their current site on Carrow Road in 1935.

The Canaries

Norwich City Football Club's original nickname was the Citizens, superseded in 1907 by the more familiar Canaries. Although there is evidence of a canary being embroidered into the shirt much earlier, the famous canary badge of Norwich City FC was adopted in 1923–24 when the shirt colour was white, with blue shorts and socks.

The First Eleven Players of Norwich City FC

The first match ever played by Norwich City FC was a friendly played on the ground at Newmarket Road against Harwich & Parkeston FC on 6 September 1902 – the result was a 1–1 draw. The players were:

1. George Bardwell
2. Robert Collinson (the first captain of the team)
3. Bill Cracknell
4. Walter Crome
5. Tommy Newell
6. Bertie Playford
7. Jimmy Shields
8. William 'Dillo' Sparkes
9. Fred Witham
10. George 'Geno' Yallop
11. Jack Yallop

Norwich Football Facts

Celebrity supporters of the Canaries include Hugh Jackman and Myleene Klass.

The first Norwich City hat-trick in a FA Cup match was achieved by Percy 'Putt' Gooch when he made his first appearance for City in a match against Lowestoft Town on 19 September 1903.

The first match to take place at The Nest was a friendly against Fulham, played on the 1 September 1908. City christened their new home ground with a 2–1 victory.

Brothers Bill and John Duncan made their debuts for City on the same day in a match against Swansea Town on 16 September 1920. Sadly, this away match ended in a 5–2 defeat.

Norwich's record victory is a 10–2 win over Coventry City in 1930.

The first Norwich City player to win an international cap was Mick O'Brien when he played for Ireland on 11 May 1930.

The Canaries have never won the FA Cup but have reached the semi-final of the competition on three occasions – in 1959, 1989 and 1992.

The Canaries won the League Cup in only its second season, beating Rochdale in the 1962 final 4–0 on aggregate.

Goalkeeper Kevin Keelan, a man recognised for his flair for fashion, owned his own boutique in Anglia Square in the 1970s.

Norwich's first shirt sponsors were local firm Poll & Withey Windows in 1983.

David Beckham had a trial for Norwich City when he was just 11. Sadly for Canaries fans, he had already decided he was going to sign for Manchester United.

TV cook Delia Smith CBE has been a joint majority shareholder (with her husband Michael Wynn-Jones) of Norwich City Football Club since 1996. They were joined on the board of directors by actor, writer and witty TV personality Stephen Fry in August 2010.

When Craig Bellamy scored a goal against his old team on the 1 February 2014, the former Canary earned himself the distinction of becoming the first player in Premier League history to score for seven different clubs.

NORWICH SPEEDWAY

The home of motorcycle speedway in Norwich was the Firs Stadium on Aylsham Road. The first race meeting to be held there took place on Sunday, 17 August 1930. The Firs began as a grass track but was soon converted and the first proper dirt track meeting held there was on 13 September 1931 between Norwich and Staines. The match was won by Norwich 33–21. The home team was the Norwich Stars, among them many outstanding riders, notably Ove Fundin who was recognised as the best rider in the world in 1958; indeed, he won the World Championship on a total of four occasions. The Firs site was sold for redevelopment to a property company on 3 March 1964.

9

TRANSPORT

TRAVELLING IN AND AROUND NORWICH

The first turnpike road to run from the city was created between Norwich and Attleborough in 1707.

A coach from Norwich to London was established in July 1761. The journey, which had previously taken two days in summer and three in winter, could now be performed in around twenty hours.

The first hackney coach in Norwich was set up by William Huggins in December 1764.

The turnpike road from Ber Street Gates, Norwich to New Buckenham was constructed in 1772. In 1794 a turnpike road linked Norwich and Aylsham and in 1796 another went to North Walsham.

The first balloon ascent to be seen in Norwich was staged at Quantrell's Gardens on 16 February 1784. Several years later, Aeronaut Mr Grais made a balloon ascent from the Newmarket Road Cricket Ground and, upon attaining an altitude of about 3,000ft, descended by means of a parachute.

In 1785, mail coaches between Norwich and London were established. They could make the journey of 108 miles in fifteen hours.

In 1802, the Lord Nelson Coach ran from the Globe Inn at King's Lynn, to the King's Head, Norwich, every Monday, Wednesday and Friday, returning Tuesday, Thursday and Saturday at 7 a.m. The journey took seven hours each way.

In the forty years after passing the 1806 Paving Act, those responsible for the task got deep into debt and left Norwich the worst paved city in England.

The first Norwich, Aylsham and Cromer coach commenced running on 23 April 1810. It ran from No. 21 Lobster Lane in Norwich to the Red Lion Inn, Cromer on Mondays, Wednesdays and Fridays and returned on Tuesdays, Thursdays and Saturdays. The proprietor of the service was Mr W. Spanton.

An exhibition of the earliest form of bicycle, known as the Pedestrian Hobby Horse, was made in Norwich in April 1819.

The first motor car appeared in Norwich in 1896, driven by theatre impresario Frederick William Fitt.

In 1911, the cost of reconstructing and surface tarring 90,465yrds of the Norwich to Thetford road was the grand sum of £6,732.

On 26 August 1927, Messrs Duff, Morgan and Vermont registered the 10,000th car in Norwich. It had the number plate of VG 1.

In November 1934, Francis Dusgate received the first fine for unlawful hooting of a motor horn during unsociable hours in Norwich. The fine was £1.

The first trial flight bringing mail to Norwich by helicopter took place on 21 February 1949. A British European Airways helicopter left Westwood airfield, Peterborough and reached Norwich within forty minutes.

RAC patrolman Arthur Coleman of Elm Grove Lane retired in March 1961 after forty years of unbroken service during which he travelled over 800,000 miles without an accident.

Commuters were up in arms in 1971 when return rail fares from Norwich to London were raised from £3.80 to £4.40.

WHEN BALLOON ASCENTS GO BAD …

On 24 November 1783, following an advertisement in Norwich newspapers, a crowd estimated to number more than 6,000 gathered on Mousehold Heath to watch the ascent of a hot air balloon with a cat, dog and pigeon in its basket. There was no balloon nor animals to be seen – the whole thing been a hoax.

A Mr Steward received short shrift in 1815 when he ascended in a balloon from the Prussia Gardens. After rising about 150ft from the ground the balloon fell and did not rise again. The disappointed and unsympathetic crowd seized upon the flaccid bladder, tore it to pieces and roughly handled the aeronaut.

THE NORWICH WHERRY

In the mid-nineteenth century, when the Wensum was far more a working river, the craft most commonly employed was the

Norwich Wherry. This craft was described in the nineteenth-century publication *The Land We Live In* as 'a light barge of from twenty to forty tons burden; it has a mast so balanced as to be raised or depressed with great ease and carried a large sail. It tacks readily, seems easily held in hand and is managed without difficulty by man and boy, or, as is quite as common, a man and his wife.'

On 23 February 1949, the Norfolk Wherry Trust was formed at a meeting in Norwich with the aim of preserving one or more of the old wherries that formerly carried most of the inland water transport of Norfolk. The trustees elected were Lady Mayhew, Mr Hector Read and Mr Lewis Storey.

THREE RAILWAY STATIONS

The construction of the first railway in Norfolk by the Eastern Counties Railway saw the arrival of Thorpe Station (Norwich Thorpe). The first sods of earth, in preparation for the construction of this line, were lifted at Postwick Hall Farm, near Thorpe Asylum, on 20 April 1843. Opened on 30 April 1844, the railway spanned 20 miles and connected Norwich and Great Yarmouth. The Great Eastern Railway took over the railway line and their magnificent new station, erected a short distance away, was opened for inspection on 1 May 1886 and used by the public for the first time on the 3rd. It has had a number of refits but the great building remains and serves the city to this day.

Victoria Station, situated between St Stephen's Road, Queen's Road and Grove Road, was built on the site of the Ranelagh Gardens by the Eastern Union Railway Company and opened on 12 December 1849. Later taken over by the Great Eastern Railway, it closed to passengers

on 22 May 1916. It finally closed as a coal depot in January 1966 and today the old station site is occupied by a Sainsbury's supermarket.

Norwich City Station at Heigham was built by the Lynn and Fakenham Railway and opened on 2 December 1882. It later became the southern terminus of the Midland and Great Northern Railway line from Melton Constable. Suffering terrible fire damage during the Baedeker Blitz of 1942, the station was never properly rebuilt; it closed to passengers on 2 March 1959 and to goods traffic in 1969. Today the site has been used for industrial units and shopping outlets.

THE THORPE RAILWAY DISASTER

The Thorpe Railway Disaster occurred on 10 September 1874 when the 9.10 p.m. express train from Norwich collided head-on with the 8.40 p.m. mail train from Great Yarmouth at Thorpe St Andrew due to human error in the signalling. Both drivers and firemen were killed, as were seventeen passengers and seventy-five people were injured. The dead and dying were removed to Field's boathouse and to the Tuns Inn, while the injured were taken to the Norfolk and Norwich Hospital where six of them later died from their injuries.

Fatalities of the Disaster
- John Prior (49), engine driver (Yarmouth Train),
  Great Eastern Railway
- Thomas Clarke (40), engine driver (Norwich Train),
  Great Eastern Railway
- James Light (25), fireman, Great Eastern Railway, Lowestoft
- Frederick Sewell (35), fireman, Great Eastern Railway, Lowestoft
- George Page, Magdalen Street, Norwich, currier (leather seller)
- G.R. Womack, Dove Street, Norwich, clothier
- Revd Henry Stacey (56), Norwich, Independent minister
- Mrs Mary Ann Stacey, Norwich, wife of Revd Henry Stacey
- Sergeant Major Cassell, Norwich, West Norfolk Militia
- Sergeant Ward, Norwich, West Norfolk Militia
- Susan Lincoln (35), Thorpe Hamlet, Norwich, housemaid
- Miss Mary Anne Murray (25), Mariner's Lane, Norwich
- Mr Russell Skinner (40), Norwich, gentleman
- Miss Mary Ann Taylor (46), Norwich, forewoman at
  Mr Caley's draper
- Mrs Sarah Gilding (38), Mile End Road, London
- Flora Gilding, Mile End Road, London (daughter of the above)

- John Betts, stoker, Great Eastern Railway, Mariner's Lane, Norwich
- Mrs Elizabeth Betts (29), wife of the above
- Infant child of Mr and Mrs Betts
- Susan Browne (33), St Benedict's, Norwich, seamstress
- Mr John Job Hupton, Great Yarmouth
- Mr Stanley Slade (25), Regent Street, London, auctioneer
- Mr Bransby Francis (59), Norwich, surgeon
- Mrs Charlotte Coote (40), London
- John Beart (61), Aldborough, Suffolk, draper

WHAT GOES AROUND ...

The horse-drawn Norwich Omnibus Company Limited was formed in May 1879 and the first omnibuses started on the Dereham Road route on 23 June the same year. It eventually wound up its affairs on 15 November 1899 in consequence of the approaching completion of the tramways scheme. The new, motorised Norwich Omnibus Company bought out Norwich Tramways in 1935 and replaced them with bus services, which they were soon operating over 36 route miles around the city with eighty-eight vehicles and 350 employees.

NORWICH TRAMWAYS

The first trial trip over the completed portion of the Norwich Electric Tramways was run on 19 April 1900. The overhead wires erected by the Tramway Company were inspected on 12 June by Mr A.P. Trotter, electric adviser to the Board of Trade and, on 26 July, Colonel Yorke of the Railway Department of the Board of Trade made an inspection of 22 miles of route on about 16 miles of roads. On 30 July 1900, the Norwich Electric Tramways Company opened its lines as a public tram system with 19 miles, 2 furlongs, 100yds of rail; a project which had cost £330,000 to install. The cars ran over the Magdalen Road, Earlham Road, Dereham Road and Thorpe Road routes. Some 25,000 people tried their first journey on a Norwich tram for the very first time on this day. The Newmarket Road route was opened later on 9 August, and the Unthank Road route on 22 December.

Bought out and replaced by a bus service, the last tram in Norwich ran on 10 December 1935. It was manned by Mr G. Hill, the company's most senior driver who was joined by their youngest employee Mr B. Fisher. The last journey ran from Orford Place to the tram sheds on Silver Road.

THE ZEPPELIN SCARESHIP MYSTERY

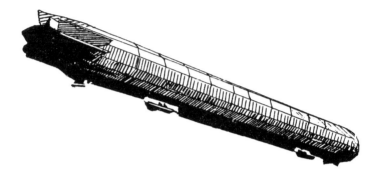

In May 1909, newspapers across Britain were full of accounts of unexplained airships seen and heard traversing the night sky over Great Britain from locations as far apart as Wales to Suffolk. To put this event into context, the Wright brothers had only achieved powered flight in 1903, Bleriot would not fly across the Channel until 25 July 1909 and the first Channel crossings by airship were a year away. In other words, no aircraft had been recorded crossing the Channel up to that time. On Wednesday, 19 May 1909, Mrs Turner of New Catton had her attention grabbed by 'a flash of light which made the street look like day' followed by a noise like 'the whirring of wheels'. She continued: 'I looked up and there I saw a big star of light in front and a big searchlight behind ... It was coming from the NNE from the direction of the Angel Road School and flying very low, so low that it would have touched the pinnacle of the school had it passed directly over it.' Mr E.B. Nye of Norwich told reporters that while others saw an airship at 11.30 p.m., he and several others saw 'a bright light in the sky, which looked exactly like a falling star' adding, 'Had our brains been inoculated with the present airship scare, we might even have heard a whizzing noise, or had a searchlight directed upon us.'

Many questions raised by these mystery airship sightings still remain over 100 years later and those from 1909, before the Channel had been officially crossed by any flying machine, are by far the most enigmatic. No evidence has yet been uncovered in the German archives or from British intelligence to prove covert missions had been undertaken by Zeppelins over Britain under the cloak of darkness in 1909. So, what did the people see? It is clear that far more people saw the airships and lights than just those who gave their names and stories to the newspapers. Could all these witnesses really be mistaken or deluded? Perhaps Britain had been gripped by a mass panic or, tantalisingly, was there more to the mystery 'scareships' over Britain in those spring skies of 1909?

CROWN POINT STATION

Extensive arrangements were made by the Great Eastern Railway to deal with the huge numbers of passenger and goods traffic travelling to and from the Royal Agricultural Show that was held at Crown Point in June 1911. The showground was situated near Trowse Station and a new temporary station, called Crown Point, was specially erected between Trowse and Whitlingham Junction for the event. It consisted of two timber platforms, each 700ft long and 18ft wide, and – on the Wensum curve near Wensum Junction – a further 2.5 miles of sidings were laid close to the new station, including two cattle-loading docks with roads on either side.

IN THE AIR

In an early security measure under the new Aerial Navigation Act, Home Secretary Winston Churchill issued an order that the navigation of aircraft of every description or any place within 4 miles of Norwich was prohibited during King George V's visit on 28 June 1911. Any person contravening the order was liable to be imprisoned for six months or face a fine of £200 – or both!

In 1923, Daimler Airways created regular flights from London to Norwich and from the Midlands to Norwich. A successful trial flight of the route between London and Norwich was flown on Saturday, 25 August 1923, using one of the new Napier DH 34 aeroplanes that were to be used on the service. Flights between London and Norwich were covered in eighty-five minutes while the Manchester to Norwich flight was two hours. Today, on average, it should be one hour and five minutes.

The Norwich and Norfolk Aero Club was formed at Mousehold Heath airfield in 1927.

The first letter delivered in Norwich by airmail was for Mr C.F. Solomon, St John's House, Ber Street on 15 May 1931.

In June 1933, the Norwich Municipal Aerodrome on Mousehold Heath was opened by the Prince of Wales (later Edward VIII).

The first Public Schools Aviation Camp in England, for boys aged 17 and over, was laid on by the Norfolk and Norwich Aero Club in August 1934. For the inclusive fee of £30, the boys received tented accommodation, food and at least twelve hours of flying time over a period of four weeks. They were expected to acquire sufficient skills to enable them to take their amateur pilots' licences.

TITANIC CONNECTIONS

RMS *Titanic* carried two passengers who were born and bred in Norwich: newlyweds Mr Edward Beane (aged 32) and his bride Ethel Beane (née Clarke). Edward Beane had moved to New York, where he worked as a bricklayer, and returned to his home city to marry Ethel shortly before they departed as second-class passengers aboard *Titanic* to start a new life together in the USA. On 14 April 1912, the ship struck an iceberg and, as it began to sink, Ethel was given a place in Lifeboat 13. In an interview shortly after the sinking, she stated that she had seen members of the ship's crew holding men back from the lifeboat stations at gunpoint after the order was given for only women and children to board the boats.

Edward Beane jumped from *Titanic* as it sank and, after some time in the water, he was pulled into Lifeboat 13 by his wife. Ethel would recall: 'We must have been a mile away in the rowboat when the *Titanic* went down. We could hear the band playing and then just before the crash of sinking the anguished cries of those on board which was like one great human wail. It was years before I could forget that terrible scream.'

Rescued by the Cunard liner RMS *Carpathia*, the couple had all of their savings and all sixty-five of their wedding presents go down with *Titanic*. The couple did settle in Rochester, New York and raised a family but never went on an ocean-going ship again.

The other Norwich connection is Mr Thomas Henry Towler Case, barrister at law of Lincoln's Inn, who acted as legal adviser to the Admiralty during the official enquiry into the loss of *Titanic*. Case was educated at Norwich Grammar School and made his home in Norwich (he died there in 1933).

BEGINNING OF THE END OF STEAM

An hourly service of diesel-hauled express trains between London and Norwich via Ipswich was put into operation on 5 January 1959. Every third train was 'extra fast', covering the 116 miles in 120 minutes. The first all-electric train arrived at Norwich in 1987.

HOW THINGS HAVE CHANGED

In January 1961, a scheme to introduce car parking meters in central areas of Norwich was rejected by the city Car Parks Committee on the grounds that 'it would not be fair to motorists'.

10

DEATH AND RELIGION

DIOCESE OF NORWICH

The origins of the Diocese of Norwich can be traced back to the seventh century when St Felix first fixed his see at Dunwich and then moved to Elmham in 673. It was thence moved to Thetford in 1070 and finally to Norwich ahead of the new cathedral building in 1094. Fifty-seven churches stood within the city wall of Norwich during the Middle Ages; thirty-one of them still exist today.

THE FIRST TEN BISHOPS OF NORWICH

(And their year of appointment)

1. Herbert de Losinga   (1094)
2. Everard of Calne   (1121)
3. William de Turbeville   (1146)
4. John of Oxford   (1175)
5. John de Gray   (1200)
6. Pandulph Masca   (1215)
7. Thomas de Blundeville   (1226)
8. Simon of Elmham   (1236)
9. William de Raleigh   (1239)
10. Walter Calthorp   (1245)

CHILD MARTYR

St William of Norwich was a popular rather than a formal papal canonisation. The boy was claimed to have been martyred by Jews in mockery of Christ's crucifixion on Mousehold Heath in 1144. His bones were retained in a shrine at Norwich Cathedral. Thomas of Monmouth, a Norwich Benedictine monk, recorded the incident and the wonders performed by St William's remains in *The Life and Miracles of St William of Norwich* (1173).

NORWICH CATHEDRAL

Norwich Cathedral's original spire was constructed in wood and was burnt down by townsmen during rioting in 1272. Rebuilt, again in wood, it was blown down in the great hurricane of 1362. A third wooden spire was struck by lightning in 1463. The stone spire we know today dates from 1480 and, despite a lightning strike damaging 20ft of the upper part of it in 1601, it was repaired and stands as the second highest spire in England at 315ft (96m), the tallest being Salisbury Cathedral.

In September 1843, a platform was erected on the summit of the spire of Norwich Cathedral by a party of sappers and miners, to support an observatory for the purpose of the trigonometrical survey then being made throughout the kingdom.

Norwich Cathedral has 1,106 carved roof bosses, each one decorated with a theological image. The nave vault shows the history of the world from the creation while the cloister includes a series showing the life of Christ and the Apocalypse. The roof bosses of Norwich Cathedral have been described as 'without parallel in the Christian world'.

DIVINE LOVE

Sixteen Revelations of Divine Love (1393) by Mother Julian of Norwich was the first book to be written by a woman in English.

ST GILES CHURCH

The church of St Giles is built in the Perpendicular style and would have been erected around 1400, although the parish itself is mentioned in Domesday Book. The 120ft church tower is the highest in Norwich and also rises from the highest point in the city.

ST JOHN MADDERMARKET

Built in the fifteenth century, at a time when Norwich was one of the richest cities in Europe, the graveyard at St John Maddermarket includes the Crabtree headstone, which has the pre-Christian symbol of the Ouroboros (a serpent eating its own tail) carved upon it.

SIR THOMAS ERPINGHAM

The magnificent Erpingham Gate, along with the choir stalls inside the cathedral, was built in 1420. Created by Sir Thomas Erpingham, the loyal knight of Henry V who led the English archers to victory at Agincourt in 1415, the gate was built as a mark of thanksgiving for this victory. Erpingham's kneeling figure, complete with snowy white hair and beard, and sword by his side, is believed to have once stood on his tomb in the cathedral but now rests in the niche directly over the gateway.

ST PETER MANCROFT

The largest church in Norwich is St Peter Mancroft, built between 1430 and 1455 on the site of a Norman church which stood in the *magna crofta* (great field) of the castle – hence the name Mancroft. Its tower is 102ft high and contains a magnificent peal of twelve bells.

The organ of St Peter Mancroft was played for the first time on 8 June 1707.

SOME OF THE LOST CHURCHES OF NORWICH

- All Saints, Fyebridge Street, on the corner of Cowgate, was taken down in 1550.
- St Buttulph's, Magdalen Street, was taken down in 1548.
- St Cuthbert's, situated towards the north end of King Street near Tombland, was demolished in 1530.
- St Martin's in Ballivia, situated near Golden Ball Lane, was demolished in 1562.
- St Olave's or St Tooley's, which stood on the east side of Tooley Street, next to the north corner of Cherry Lane, was demolished in 1546.
- St Michael at Thorn on Ber Street was gutted during the Baedeker Blitz of 1942 and was subsequently demolished.
- St Paul's church on Barrack Street was gutted during the Baedeker Blitz of 1942. The ruins remained for some years after until it was finally demolished to make way for the inner link road.
- St Benedict's church on St Benedict's Street was gutted during the Baedeker Blitz of 1942. The walls of the body of the church were subsequently demolished and the scarred tower was left as a gaunt reminder of the Blitz on the city.

A BISHOP IN TURBULENT TIMES

Bishop Joseph Hall (1574–1656) one of Britain's first satirists, a man imprisoned in the Tower of London by the Commons for speaking out about the conduct of the government, served as Bishop of Norwich from 1641 but was removed from his beloved cathedral by Commonwealth forces in 1643 and had to watch its desecration. He described the sight in his tract *Hard Measure*:

Lord, what work was here; what clattering of glasses, what beating down of walls, what tearing up of monuments, what pulling down of seats, what wresting out of irons and brass from the widows and graves, what defacing of armes, what demolishing of curious stone which had not any representation in the world, but only the cast of the founder, and the skill of the mason, what toting and piping upon the destroyed organ pipes and what a hideous triumph on the market day, before all the country, when in a sacriligious and profane procession, all the organ pipes, vestments, both copes and surplices, together with the leaden cross which had been newly sawn down from over the green yard pulpit and the service book and the singing books that could be had, were carried to a fire in a public market place; a lewd wretch walking before the train in his cope, trailing in the dirt, with a service book in his hand, imitating in an impious scorn the tune and usurping the words of the Litany; the ordnance being discharged on the guild day, the Cathedral was filled with musketeers, drinking and tobaccoing, as freely as if it had turned alehouse.

Bishop Hall continued to preach in the city whenever he could obtain the use of a pulpit. He would live at the Bishop's Palace in Heigham until his death in 1656 and was buried in the nearby church of St Bartholomew.

THE FIRST IN THE FIRING LINE!

In 1574, Norwich was so notorious for its Nonconformity that, when orders were given to Archbishop Parker to 'Punish the Puritan Ministers', Queen Elizabeth I gave him private orders to begin with Norwich. Accordingly, in 1576, many of the Norwich ministers were suspended and treated so severely that even the county justices presented a petition to Her Majesty praying for leniency towards them.

BROWNISTS

Robert Browne was the first seceder from the Church of England and the first to found a Church of his own on Congregational principles. Settling in the city in 1580, by the following year he had attempted to set up a separate Church in Norwich. This proved popular and his followers became commonly known as Brownists. From this foundation developed the Congregational Church. However, he and his followers suffered persecution and it is claimed that Browne was arrested and imprisoned thirty-two times for his Nonconformist beliefs. Browne died while in Northampton Gaol in 1633.

THE OLD MEETING HOUSE, COLEGATE

William Bridge, rector of St Peter Hungate and curate of St George's Tombland, was removed from his position for refusing to read James I's *Book of Sports*. He joined the early Congregationalists in the city and fled with a number of them to Holland to escape persecution. Others sailed for America, where they helped to found the City of Norwich, Connecticut. Bridge returned to Norwich and founded his congregation in 1642 and it was their successors that built the Meeting House in 1693. Even at this time it was feared their faith would come under attack and the Meeting House was built in a courtyard so that the men of the congregation could defend the entry against rioters, while the women and children got out at the back.

WHAT A WAY TO GO!

Former Norwich mayor, Adrian Parmenter, the man who built the first Norwich Office of the Excise in 1643, died in 1663 from rabies contracted after a bite from a mad fox.

On 18 February 1832, Thomas Foyson (53) proprietor of the Calvert Street Vinegar Works in Norwich fell into a vat of vinegar he was gauging and drowned.

At a convivial night at the Three Turks at Charing Cross, Norwich, in October 1835, local artisan William Cork was singing the song composed upon the death of General Wolfe and after repeating the words 'And I to death must yield' he instantly fell down and died.

Mr Walter Morgan of Morgan's Brewery on King Street, Norwich, met his death by falling into a vat of beer in May 1845.

When a boiler exploded at the brewery of Messrs Arnold and Wyatt, St Margaret's Plain, Norwich, on 12 March 1866, engine driver William Whitworth was killed in the blast when his body was hurled into the beck containing six quarters of boiling wort.

John Gurney of Sprowston Hall, Deputy Mayor of Norwich, retired from the office of mayor of the city in November 1886 and sought relaxation on the shores of the Mediterranean. The severe shock of an earthquake, which occurred at Cannes at the time of his visit, is supposed to have told upon his highly sensitive nerves and indirectly caused his death in February 1887.

Old campaigner Major Dods of the Norfolk Regiment, who had served in India, Gibraltar and Burma, finally succumbed to the blazing sun in the garden of his Thorpe St Andrew home and died of heatstroke during the heatwave of 1911.

Terence Barclay, the eldest son of Mr Hugh Barclay of Colney Hall, died in December 1911 after he was fatally clawed by one of his father's pet lions.

George Martin (62), a roadman from Framingham Earl, was crushed to death by a steamroller in Norwich on 15 April 1920.

Lieutenant Colonel J.R. Harvey DSO (Distinguished Service Order), a former Mayor of Norwich who had a command in Palestine during the First World War, was found dead in the garden of his house in Thorpe St Andrew in July 1921, having accidentally discharged his gun while getting over a wire fence.

In a case brought before the Norwich district coroner in July 1957, it was found a Boy Scout was killed by shock when lightning struck the bell tent he was staying in as he was scraping out a tin of treacle.

REST IN PEACE

Sir Thomas Browne, the notable Norwich physician and philosopher, was not allowed to rest in peace after his death in October 1682. His grave was discovered while preparing another in the sanctuary of St Peter Mancroft church in Norwich in 1840; after a brief examination most of him was reburied, with the exception of his skull, hair and coffin plate, which were removed by local chemist Robert Fitch. Later presented by a Dr Lubbock to the Norfolk and Norwich Hospital, it was displayed in their museum for many years afterwards until 1922 when eventually, after an undignified squabble about its cost and value, the skull was finally reinterred in a specially made casket with full burial rites that referred to it being 317 years old!

DOOM YEAR FOR THE MAYORS

In the year 1717, Norwich lost two mayors – Richard Lubbock and Thomas Bubbin – while they were serving office. I bet Anthony Parmenter, who saw the year out as mayor, was praying it would not be three in a row!

THE OCTAGON

Built in 1756 to replace an old Presbyterian meeting house, the Octagon is a masterwork by noted Norwich architect Thomas Ivory. John Wesley described it as the most elegant meeting house in Europe but added disapprovingly, 'How can it be thought that the old course gospel should find admission here?' In the early nineteenth century, the congregation became Unitarian and remains so to this day.

FAREWELL TO THE SMITH

On a gravestone erected by John Dixon for his father Owen, the Old Catton blacksmith who died 17 October 1758, is the following epitaph:

My sledge and hammer lay reclin'd,
My bellows too have lost their wind,
My fire's extinct, my forge decayed,
And in the dust my vice is laid,
My coal is spent, my iron's gone,
My nails are all drove, my work is done.

NORWICH CEMETERIES

Norwich-born Unitarian minister Thomas Drummond (1764–1852) was the founder of the Rosary – the first nondenominational cemetery in England. When he died he was buried alongside his wife in the cemetery he had created.

The Lord Bishop of Norwich consecrated the new Norwich cemetery at Earlham on 27 February 1856. Land amounting to 35 acres had been purchased by the Board of Health from Mr John Cater, but only 23 acres were at first utilised. The buildings were erected by Messrs Ling and Balls, from designs by Mr Benest, the city surveyor, at a cost of £1,990.

SUNDAY SCHOOL

The first Sunday school in Norwich was established in St Stephen's in 1785.

THAT'S MY PEW

In December 1844, Edward Stracey, of St Peter Mancroft, Norwich, was taken to court regarding the tenancy of a pew in the parish church. He was taken into custody and lodged in the jail, due to his refusal to pay the costs imposed by the Norwich Ecclesiastical Court.

REVD JAMES BROWN

The Revd James Brown, Hon. Canon of Norwich, was vicar of St Andrew's church for fifty years. He also served as chaplain to the county prison for over twenty years and was in attendance to deliver the final sermon and rites at almost every public execution during that time. He died on 1 October 1856 in his 83rd year.

BY THE WAY ...

The Independent Congregational Chapel in the Field, with its twin turrets each standing 80ft high, was often erroneously believed to be the chapel from which Chapel Field Gardens takes its name. Opened for public worship on 30 September 1858 by the Revd Newman Hall LL.B, the chapel was erected, at the cost of £3,000, by Mr Horace Sexton from the plans of Mr Joseph James, architect of Furnival's Inn, and was intended to accommodate a congregation of 1,000. The last service was held there on 30 December 1966 and the chapel was sadly demolished in 1972.

TROUBLESOME PRIEST

Joseph Leycester Lyne, the self-styled 'Brother' or 'Father' Ignatius, took to wearing a monk's habit and established his own form of Benedictine 'monastery' on Elm Hill in 1863, which he bought with the proceeds of a speaking tour he had made across England and Wales. He was claimed, by some, to have performed miracles and he attracted both support and controversy. Within three years the 'monastery' was closed and Ignatius was driven out of the city amid allegations of fraud and degenerate behaviour. He returned to Norwich and preached to large audiences every time he came, but one does wonder if they attended more through curiosity than faith.

ALL GAS AND GAITERS

The Revd Henry Rumsey and several members of the choir were at practice when a disastrous gas explosion occurred at the church of St John Maddermarket, Norwich, in September 1875. Rumsey, with a lighted taper in his hand, was in the act of turning off the gas at one of the standards when a brilliant flame shot across the north side of the nave, followed by a terrible explosion which completely wrecked the interior of the church. The choir escaped without injury but Rumsey was hurled a distance of several yards and severely shaken and bruised. The damage was estimated at £1,000.

A FEW ADDITIONS

Prince's Street Sunday schools and Norwich Lecture Hall were opened as an adjunct to the Congregational church on 17 January 1881. The fine block of buildings was designed by Mr Edward Boardman, architect, and erected by Messrs Downing and Sons at the cost of about £12,600.

THE SALVATION ARMY

General William Booth, founder of the Salvation Army, made his first visit to Norwich on 9 August 1882.

On 14 March 1892, the memorial stones of a permanent building to be used as the headquarters of the Salvation Army in Norwich were laid by Mr George White and other prominent Nonconformists in St Giles Street. The building, which, inclusive of the site, cost about £4,000, was opened on 30 October.

CATHOLIC CONFERENCE

The third National Roman Catholic Conference was held in Norwich in August 1912.

ON THE AIR

An experiment of a church service conducted entirely by wireless was successfully achieved at St Bartholomew's church, Heigham, on the evening of Sunday, 12 July 1925 when they heard a sermon broadcast from St Martin-in-the-Fields, Trafalgar Square, London.

SEE THE POINTS

It was only discovered in 1932 that the four pinnacles at the corners of the tower of Norwich Cathedral were placed symmetrically by the medieval builders with regard to the diagonals of the tower. The discovery was made by Mr C.H. Gale of Diss, a fellow of the Royal Institute of British Architects who, during a casual visit to the cathedral, happened to notice something odd about the pinnacles.

ABBEY OF FÉCAMP

In readiness for the celebration of the foundation of the Abbey of Fécamp, Normandy, on 31 July 1932, an oblong stone – presumed to have been in one of the walls of the Lady chapel of Norwich Cathedral, pulled down in the reign of Elizabeth I – was sent by the dean and chapter of Norwich to be incorporated in the fabric of the abbey.

This was in honour of Herbert de Losinga, who had been a monk at Fécamp and served as prior of the abbey before he became the first Bishop of Norwich.

AT SEA

In July 1956, Miss Dorothy Diggens of Unthank Road was buried at sea in deference to a request made in her will. Miss Diggens, who died aged 61, had no seafaring associations but asked to be buried at sea because she did not like the idea of being placed in a coffin.

CATHOLIC CATHEDRAL

The Roman Catholic cathedral church of St John the Baptist in Norwich was only consecrated as a cathedral church in 1976. Built on the site of the Norwich City Gaol between 1882 and 1910, to designs by George Gilbert Scott Junior, it was originally opened as the church of St John the Baptist on 8 December 1910.

11

IN SICKNESS
AND IN HEALTH

The Great Hospital does not really owe its foundation to Henry VIII as stated upon the inscription set into its outer wall. This inscription alludes to the fact that Henry handed the building over to the city upon the dissolution of the cathedral priory instead of selling it to swell the royal coffers. St Helen's Hospital was founded by Bishop Walter de Suffield in 1249 and chartered for the maintenance of 'poor and decrepit chaplains' and for the support of thirteen poor people and seven poor scholars of the grammar school.

When the Black Death hit Norwich in 1349, the city is believed to have lost two-fifths of its population and at least half of its clergy.

When the well-known apothecary drug jar makers Jasper Andries and Jacob Janson migrated from Antwerp in 1550 they first came to Norwich, before being granted permission by Elizabeth I to set up a pottery in London.

A record known as the Norwich Roll claims that some of the staff and vehicles that brought Elizabeth I to Norwich in August 1578 were infected with plague and spread the killer disease. During the course of the following year and three-quarters, over one-third of the population of Norwich would die.

Plague returned to Norwich in 1626 and killed 1,430 people. It came again in 1630 and a pest house was erected near the great tower on Butler's Hills. In 1636, plague was once more recorded in the city but fewer people died. In 1665, 2,251 people died and, rolling on into 1666, a further 699 people succumbed.

In 1669, smallpox spread through 300 city families in a fortnight. It returned in 1681 and again in 1710, claiming numerous lives.

Doughty's Hospital on Calvert Street was founded in 1687 after William Doughty bequeathed £6,000 for its erection and endowment as part of his will. After his death in 1688, Doughty's trustees purchased an orchard in St Saviours and arranged the building of thirty-two almshouses. In 1895, it held twenty-four poor men and nineteen women, each of whom received an allowance of 5s 6d weekly with coals and a new suit of purple every year. Modernised, Doughty's Hospital today looks very much like any other sheltered housing development.

Benjamin Gooch (1708–76) was one of the founders of the Norfolk and Norwich Hospital. Along with John Harmer of Norwich, Gooch was a leading lithotomist in the first half of the eighteenth century, when bladder stones were more common in Norfolk than anywhere else in the country. He performed this potentially lethal operation to success on many occasions and made quite a lot of money from it, hence it may be said the foundations of the old Norfolk and Norwich Hospital were literally built on stone! Indeed the tradition was perpetuated by William Donne (1746–1804) – one of the first surgeons to be appointed to the hospital and who performed 170 lithotomy operations during his thirty-two years on the staff – and the celebrated surgeon John Greene Crosse (1791–1850), who also published works on the treatment of bladder stones.

Mrs Mary Chapman erected the Bethel Hospital for the Insane on Bethel Street in 1713. The hospital had been an idea of Mary and her husband Samuel Chapman, a former rector of Thorpe, both of whom had experience of psychiatric-related illness in their own families. In 1962, it was claimed that the Bethel was the oldest surviving hospital in the country specifically founded for the care of psychiatric patients, and was the oldest building to have been in continuous psychiatric use in the UK. The inpatient facilities closed in 1974 and today it has been converted into private flats.

Edward Rigby MD, who practiced as an accoucheur in the city with distinguished success from 1769, was an author of several noted works on midwifery, medicine and agriculture. He was a strenuous promoter of vaccination and worked as an assistant surgeon in the Norfolk and Norwich Hospital from its first establishment in 1771, progressing to surgeon in 1790 and physician in 1814. He died at his house in St Giles in his 74th year in 1821.

In 1771, William Fellowes and Benjamin Gooch established the Norfolk and Norwich Hospital as a charitable institution. The hospital itself was paid for by public subscription and first opened for outpatients on 11 July 1772 and to inpatients almost four months later on 7 November 1772.

A Society for Recovering Drowned People was formed at Norwich in 1774.

In the nineteenth-century, Heigham Hall in Upper Heigham was a psychiatric hospital for the treatment of ninety-five upper- and middle-class patients.

Dr Warner Wright, founder of the Norwich Dispensary, was chosen in 1804 as a physician of the Norfolk and Norwich Hospital, a position that he resigned from in 1840. For many years he was visiting physician to the Norfolk County Lunatic Asylum, and to the Norwich Bethel. Wright died in 1845 and the Norwich Dispensary on the Maddermarket was formally dissolved after 112 years, on 3 March 1916.

Sarah Pickwood of St Mary's, Norwich, died in December 1806, aged 49. She was recorded as 'one of the most enormous cases of dropsy on record'. To ease her suffering, in the course of fifty months she was tapped thirty-eight times and discharged 350 gallons of fluid.

Notable artist Henry Bright (1810–73) acted as dispenser to the Norfolk and Norwich Hospital for a number of years.

The Norfolk and Norwich Eye Infirmary was opened on Pottergate Street in 1822.

Norwich was the second city in the country to have a children's hospital – the first was London's Great Ormond Street Hospital for Children, opened in 1852. The Jenny Lind Infirmary for Sick Children was established by unanimous decision at a public meeting on 30 May 1853, with funding provided by the proceeds of two concerts performed by the 'Swedish Nightingale', which raised £1,253 for charitable purposes. The money was used to buy a house in Pottergate and convert it into a twenty-bed infirmary for sick children. The first inpatients were admitted on 3 April 1854.

Mr Cockle, the original proprietor of the antibilious pill that went by his name and who sold the recipe for several thousand pounds, died in January 1854, aged 84, at Heigham Hall psychiatric hospital in Norwich.

Dr William Guy saved many lives in Norwich when he bravely took medical charge of the isolation hospital during the smallpox outbreak in 1871. Afterwards appointed to the post of public vaccinator, it was said for years after that Norwich was 'the best vaccinated town in the kingdom'.

The Prince of Wales laid the foundation stone of the new Norfolk and Norwich Hospital on 17 June 1879. The cost of the new hospital was originally estimated at £35,500, but the Board of Governors subsequently decided to purchase adjoining property, at an additional outlay of £5,000. The Board afterwards adopted a building design jointly prepared by Mr T.H. Wyatt of London and Mr Edward Boardman, of Norwich, and accepted the tender of Messrs Lacey and Co. for the completion of the work. The new hospital was opened by the Duke and Duchess of Connaught upon its completion on 20 August 1883. The actual expenditure to that date had been £51,179. The 'N&N' closed in 2003 when services were moved to the new Norfolk and Norwich University Hospital at Colney.

The Norwich City Lunatic Asylum was erected at Hellesdon in 1880 for a total cost of about £64,000, from the designs of Mr R.M. Phipson FRIBA (Fellow of the Royal Institute of British Architects) of Norwich.

Wincarnis tonic wine, originally called Liebig's Extract of Meat and Malt Wine, was first produced under the brand name of Wincarnis by Coleman and Co. Ltd at Norwich in 1887. The product took off and the Wincarnis Works on Westwick Street produced and sent thousands of bottles all over the world every year.

The Norwich Homeopathic Dispensary stood on St Peter's Street and had around 2,000 patients in 1895.

In March 1896, Dr Thomson, medical superintendent of the Norfolk County Asylum, delivered a lecture before the Norfolk and Norwich Medico-Chirurgical Society on 'The New Photography' and presented the first practical demonstration of the Röntgen rays (X-rays) in the city.

On 3 February 1899, Mrs Elizabeth Garrett Anderson, the first woman to qualify as a physician and surgeon in Britain, delivered a lecture at Noverre's Rooms on 'The History and Effect of Vaccination'.

In February 1932, some fifty nurses and wardmaids at the Norfolk and Norwich Hospital were all suffering from influenza and, as a result, one of the wards had to be closed to ease the strain on the staff.

12

FOOD AND DRINK

SOME NORWICH TASTES OF THE PAST

- Norwich Silk Sherry from Back's, No. 3 Haymarket
- Domecq's Norwich Cream Sherry from Barwell's, No. 16 Charing Cross
- Steven's Norwich Hollow Biscuits of St Giles (good with dried Norfolk Biffin Apples)
- Coleman's Tonic Cocoa Cubes from Coleman's Works on Palace Plain
- Wincarnis Tonic Wine
- A big pizza from Bill's Pizzas on St Augustines

- A recipe shown on 'Patrick's Pantry' on *About Anglia*
- Leach's Cough Tablets bought from Billy Bluelight
- Collin's Elixir Cough Medicine from Collin's Chemist on The Walk
- Caley's Home-Brewed Ginger Beer
- Savoury or sweet pancakes from Pizza One, Pancakes Too
- Fortune Chocolate assortment from Caley's
- Steward & Patteson Ltd Ales and Stout, Pockthorpe Brewery
- Morgan's Brewery Company Ales, the Old Brewery, King Street
- Youngs, Crawshay and Youngs Norwich Ales and Stout from the Crown Brewery on King Street
- Bullard's Beers from the Anchor Brewery on Westwick Street
- Sparkling Dinner Ale from Chamberlin & Smith on Exchange Street
- Norwich Brewery Beers, King Street
- Lambert's BOP (Broken Orange Pekoe) Tea from the Mecca on Haymarket

LAMBERT'S TEAS – are the best –

F. LAMBERT AND SON LTD., NORWICH, IPSWICH and GT. YARMOUTH

SWAN

An eighteenth-century swan pit was used for the breeding and fattening of swans, some of them for the dinner table at the Great Hospital. The delicacy was enjoyed – usually with red currant jelly – at certain religious and civic dinners in the city up to the Second World War when the pit was discontinued due to rationing of feed.

NOG AND EARLY PURL

The popular commercially brewed beer in late eighteenth-century Norwich was called Nog. During the nineteenth century, the workers of the city often started their day with 'Morning' or 'Early Purl' a hot spiced beer laced with wormwood. The last pub in Norwich to have a 5 a.m. license for the benefit of early morning workers was the Great Eastern pub that stood on the corner of St Stephen's Street and Queen's Road.

ABSTAINERS

In September 1882, a three weeks' mission, in furtherance of the Blue Ribbon movement (teetotallers), was commenced in Norwich by the movement's founder, Mr Francis Murphy. The new pledges taken during the mission numbered 10,000, and upwards of 15,000 blue ribbons were distributed.

SOME UNUSUAL PUB NAMES OF NORWICH PAST

- Boarded House, Castle Ditches
- Bowling Green Tap, Theatre Street
- Boy and Cup, Pottergate Street
- Bullock and Butcher, St Giles Hill
- Cock and House, Duke Street
- Cow and Hare, Heigham Street

- Crooked Billet, Heigham Street
- Fleckered Bull, Ber Street
- Hatchett and Gate, Lower Goat Lane
- Hospital Boy, White Friar's Street
- Lame Dog, Brazen Doors
- Man Loaded with Mischief, St Paul's Back Lane
- Three Pigeons, Fishgate Street
- Tumble-down Dick, Ber Street
- Two Necked Swan, Market Place
- Whip and Egg, Tooley Street
- Wild Man, Pottergate Street

PHEASANT GALORE!

During the glut of pheasants in November 1960, shoots in the county could bag as many as 500 birds a day. In Norwich, one of the game retailers was taking 1,000 birds a day and selling them for as little as 6s a time.

CHEERS!

Norwich could once boast a number of breweries within its bounds. Most of the good old names, such as Steward and Patteson, Bullards and Morgans, are now gone, however, and even Caley's Mineral Waters are no more. Nevertheless, time moves on and today, the BLOMAX 12 Series III cavity moulding machines are capable of producing 32,000 bottles an hour. First installed at Britvic's bottling facility in the city in 2003, other even more advanced BLOMAX machines followed soon after and Norwich now packs the majority of the Robinson's ready-to-drink range and is home of the Fruit Shoot.

MANY USES FOR MUSTARD

Colman's Mustard was not just used as a hot, pungent accompaniment to meats such as beef, roast pork or cooked ham. By the late nineteenth century, it was being packaged and marketed for medical purposes, including mustard baths to revive aching muscles or treat fevers and seizures, and mustard oil for the alleviation of cold symptoms, bronchial pneumonia, pleurisy and rheumatism. Mustard poultices were also applied to the chest or abdomen to stimulate healing.

SOME GREAT TASTES OF NORWICH TODAY

- Caley's Marching Chocolate
- A Chilli Dog from the Banger Stop cart (they make their own sausages)
- A Ronaldo Ice Cream or Hot Chestnuts in the winter on London Street
- Chips off the market
- Pickerings Sausages – he makes all his own too!
- Colman's Mustard
- A cream tea at Jarrold's
- A waffle at The Waffle House on St Giles Street
- An Aldous ice cream
- Fish and chips from Valori's
- A large slice of pizza from Amaretto, St George's Street
- A vegan chickpea pancake from Frank's Bar on Bedford Street
- A light lunch at the Assembly House, Theatre Street
- Lasagna from Louis' Deli on Upper St Giles
- A burger from Zak's Mousehold Diner
- Wing of skate at Brummell's Seafood Restaurant on Magdalen Street

13

SENSE
OF PLACE

NORWICH REVIEWS

Perhaps the most profound of all the commentaries on Norwich,
especially in the light of post-war demolitions and inner link road
construction in the twentieth century, was that written by Bale in his
Continuation of Leland's Antiquities in 1549:

> Oh cytie of England, whose glory standeth more in belly chere
> than in the searche for wisdom godlye, how coeth it that neither
> you nor yet your ydell masmongers have regarded this most
> worthy commodytie of your countrye? I mean the conservacyon
> of your antiquities and of the worthy labours of your learned men.

In his *The Worthies of England* (1662), Thomas Fuller wrote of Norwich
that it was:

> Either a city in an orchard or an orchard in a city, so equally are
> houses and trees blended in it, so that the pleasure of the country
> and the populousness of the city meet here together. Yet in this
> mixture, the inhabitants participate nothing of the rusticalness of
> the one, but altogether the urbanity and civility of the other.

Traveller, diarist and miscellanist John Evelyn (1620–1706) wrote of
Norwich in a letter to Sir Thomas Browne, 'I hear Norwich is a place
very much addicted to the flowery part.'

Sir Thomas Brown wrote in 1662: 'Let any stranger find me out so
pleasant a county such good ways, large heaths, three such places as
Norwich, Yarmouth and Lynn, in any county of England, and I'll be
once again a vagabond and visit to them.'

In his *Tour Through the Whole Island of Great Britain* (1724), Daniel Defoe wrote of the city: 'The inhabitants being all busy at their manufactures, dwell in their garrets at their looms, in their combing-shops, so they all them [*sic*], twisting-mills, and other work-houses; almost all the works they are employed in being done within doors.'

The phrase Norwich 'a fine city' is taken from George Borrow's semi-autobiographical novel *Lavengro* (1851), which depicted Norwich as:

> A fine old city, perhaps the most curious specimen at present extant of the genuine old English Town … There it spreads from north to south, with its venerable houses, its numerous gardens, its thrice twelve churches, its mighty mound … There is an old grey castle on top of that mighty mound: and yonder rising three hundred feet above the soil, from amongst those noble forest trees, behold that old Norman master-work, that cloud-enriched cathedral spire … Now who can wonder that the children of that fine old city are proud, and offer up prayers for her prosperity?

A DUKE'S DISPLEASURE

Thomas Howard, 3rd Duke of Norfolk, built his palace by the bank of the Wensum in Norwich between the years 1561 and 1563. This magnificent structure was said to be one of the finest town houses in England but in 1710, when the Mayor of Norwich refused permission for the duke's company of comedians to enter the city with trumpets and due procession, the duke was outraged. He immediately defaced his palace and ordered it to be demolished.

CANARIES OF NORWICH

It is claimed that canaries were first brought over to Norwich with the 'Strangers' (Protestant refugees from the Spanish Netherlands) in the sixteenth century, who kept them for company and entertainment in cages in their weaving garrets. Certainly one of the oldest canary types developed in England; the Norwich Canary can be white, cinnamon and variegated colours as well as the famous yellow. They are also known as John Bull canaries because of their thickset build and heavy brows. On 16 November 1846, the first recorded canary show was held in Norwich at the Greyhound Inn, Ber Street, when 300 specimens belonging to the canary club were exhibited. By the late nineteenth and early twentieth centuries, the main breeding area was Heigham, where many of the city's 3,000 breeders lived and many back gardens and yards contained an aviary. The breeders were mainly working men who supplemented their earnings as boot and shoe operatives by the sales of the birds they bred. Jacob Mackley was one of the most famous Norwich breeders who won many prizes with his birds and shipped about 10,000 Norwich canaries to New York every year.

AN EARLY BIRDCAGE

The earliest English depiction of a birdcage is believed to be the stone sculpture, dated around 1630, situated on the monument to Sir John Suckling in St Andrew's church. It is shaped like a square lantern, with an ogee-domed top; the cage door is open and the dove, representing the spirit, is about to soar.

THE EARL OF NORWICH

Sir Edward Denny was created Lord Denny de Waltham and Earl of Norwich for the great services to the state of his grandfather, Sir Anthony Denny, one of the executors of Henry VIII and guardians of Edward VI. Lord Norwich died without male issue in 1637 and his earldom became extinct. During the English Civil War, the title was revived and granted to George Goring, the nephew of the deceased earl. The title became extinct again on the death of Goring's son Charles, who died without issue in 1671. Despite attempts to petition the king for the revival of the earldom in the 1920s, the title remains extinct.

LONGEVITY

Susannah Steavenson was born on 14 December 1769, the daughter of Joshua Sabberton, a chairmaker in St George's Colegate and (according to a certificate given in 1836 by the Revd W.F. Blakewell) the then minister at the Octagon chapel. Baptised on 24 December 1769, Susannah lived in Norwich until her death in her 105th year. Active and in possession of a good memory, a few days before her death she was heard to repeat no less than thirty verses that she had learnt at school ninety-five years previously. Her daughter also lived to a good age – she mourned the loss of three husbands and was planning to marry again when she was in her late seventies.

SOME UNUSUAL SOCIETIES AND ASSOCIATIONS FROM NORWICH'S PAST

- Norfolk Book Hawking Association (established in 1855)
- Norwich Anacreontic Society (established in 1800)
- Norfolk and Norwich Institution for the Encouragement of Faithful Female Servants (established in 1824)
- Society for the Suppression of Mendicity and for the Relief of Distressed Travellers
- The Association for the Relief of Decayed Tradesmen, their Widows and Orphans (established in 1790)
- The Hole in the Wall Club
- The Female Friendly Society (established in 1802 for the benefit of women in times of sickness and old age)
- The Friars' Society for the Participation of Useful Knowledge (established in 1785)
- The Norfolk and Norwich Animal's Friend Society (established in 1840)
- The Norfolk and Norwich Auxiliary Society for the Extinction of the Slave Trade and Civilization of Africa (formed in 1840)
- The Norfolk and Norwich Society for Promoting Christianity Among Jews
- The Norwich Lying-in Society (established in 1832 for delivering poor married women)
- The Society of Universal Goodwill

REVOLUTIONARIES!

Norwich had a Revolution Club in the late eighteenth and early nineteenth centuries. Their headquarters was in the Blue Bell (now the Bell Inn) and they also met at the Queen's Arms on Elm Hill but did not like the royal connotations in its name, persuading the hostelry to change its name to the Briton's Arms!

PASS THE PORT

When passing port around the dinner table, tradition dictates that a diner should pass the decanter to the left immediately after pouring a glass for his or her neighbour on the right and that the decanter should not stop its clockwise progress around the table until it is finished. If a guest fails to follow tradition or they have failed to notice the decanter, they are politely asked, 'Do you know the Bishop of Norwich?' Those aware of the tradition treat the question as a reminder, while those who don't are told, 'He's a terribly good chap, but he always forgets to pass the port.' Exactly which bishop this relates to is debatable, but it is often attributed to Henry Bathurst, Bishop of Norwich from 1805 until his death in office in 1837. Bishop Bathurst lived to the ripe old age of 93, by which time his eyesight was deteriorating, and he had developed a tendency to fall asleep at the table towards the end of the meal. As a result, he often failed to pass on the port decanters, several of which would accumulate by his right elbow.

WIFE SELLING

On 6 May 1842, Samuel Wilkinson of Mill Street, Peafield, Lakenham, appeared before the Norwich magistrates and stated that he wished to sell his wife. The magistrates referred him to the ecclesiastical court, but he said he would effect the sale and take the risk. On the 7th, at or near the Prussia Gardens, he sold his wife for a guinea, and received a sovereign on account. On the 10th, Wilkinson was bound over to keep the peace for assaulting his wife. In the course of the hearing, the following written agreement was produced:

> This is to satfy that I Samyoul Wilkerson sold my wife to
> Mr Gorge Springle for the sum of one pound one before witness.
> Samyoul X Wilkerson
> Maryann Wilkerson X her mark
> Gorge Springle X his mark
> Frederick Cornish, witness.

UNUSUAL AND UNFORTUNATE NAMES RECORDED IN NORWICH

Cain Abel	(1842)	Mary Bummer	(1769)
Anne Arse	(1824)	Percy Buttock	(1894)
John Raspberry Balls	(1825)	Cockle Cadywold	(1800)
Christmas Bear	(1873)	Christmas Cockaday	(1848)
Roger Beast	(1472)	Kerenhappuck Cockett	(1873)
Ann Bender	(1801)	William Cockman	(1711)
Henry Bollock	(1849)	Thirza Cocksedge Bignold	(1835)
Eliza Bugg	(1896)	Mary Back Crack	(1841)
Alice Bugger	(1857)	Mary Crank	(1863)

Edward Crapper	(1895)	Noah Peascod	(1774)
Sarah Dangles	(1795)	Oliver Poop	(1699)
Ann Death	(1842)	Jehosephat Postle	(1763)
Edward Dingles	(1755)	Bathsheba Pratt	(1838)
Martha Dung	(1823)	Rachel Shite	(1841)
Jephunneh Dyer	(1861)	Martha Slut	(1754)
Henry Felcher	(1851)	Francis Smallpiece	(1622)
James Gender	(1830)	William Stains	(1861)
Thomas Gland	(1698)	Hephzibah Tinkler	(1873)
Knipe Gobbett	(1771)	Octavius Toll	(1896)
David Gook	(1842)	Sarah Wanger	(1755)
Elizabeth Gotobed	(1823)	Phoebe Winkle	(1871)
Dick Head	(1842)	Theodosia Worm	(1792)
Samuel Maggot	(1796)		

NORWICH TERRIERS

The Norwich Terrier was originally bred in East Anglia as a working dog to hunt small vermin and rodents. Although the breed has been around since the mid-nineteenth century, the Norwich Terrier was only recognised in the show ring by the Kennel Club since 1932. Today, these friendly and intelligent little dogs are mostly bred as companions. The breed has spread around the world and there are now Norwich Terrier Clubs in America, Sweden, the Netherlands and Finland.

COMET COMMENT

Donati's Comet was viewed with interest by thousands of Norwich citizens in September 1858 and many believed that the extreme heat enjoyed that month must have had something to do with the comet's appearance.

WHETHER THE WEATHER

The first annual meeting of the Norwich Meteorological Society was held at the Literary Institution on 1 July 1870. After the visit of the British Association to Norwich in 1868, the local committee, having defrayed all the expenses, had a balance in hand of upwards of £300. At a meeting of subscribers, £100 of this balance was devoted to the purchase of meteorological instruments and, on 3 December 1868, the society was formed, with Mr S. Gurney Buxton as president.

VOTES FOR WOMEN!

Suffragette leader Mrs Emmeline Pankhurt was refused a hearing at a meeting in Norwich in December 1912. She made several attempts to address the gathering but the disorder was so great that she found herself unable to continue and the meeting broke up with the audience singing the national anthem.

NORWICH LAD'S CLUB

The Norwich Lad's Club was founded in 1918 by the then chief constable of Norwich City Police, John Henry Dain. The Lad's Club worked with boys aged 14 to 18 to provide them with positive influences, activities and experiences from lectures to physical fitness at a time when criminal behaviour was seen to be particularly prevalent amongst working-class boys from deprived backgrounds. The crime rate did indeed fall and, with a nightly attendance of nearly 700 boys, the premises were extended and overhauled in 1936–37. The Lad's Club sadly closed in the 1990s and the buildings were demolished in 1997.

PHILOSOPHY OF THE BISHOP OF NORWICH

In June 1921, Bertram Pollock, the Bishop of Norwich, opened a new diocesan maternity home in Norwich. He reputedly suggested that noisy girls thought that loudness or coarseness was the best way to attract the attention of young men. This was not, the bishop stressed, the attention of young men whose love was worth having. Indeed, there was many a young man ready, to use his own phrase, to 'fool about for a bit' with a flashy girl, while all the time he regards her as the very last person he would make his wife.

A FINE SOCIETY FOR A FINE CITY

The Norwich Society was established in 1923 by a group of architects, archaeologists and citizens concerned to preserve the historically and architecturally significant buildings and structures of the city so that they would not be swept away unnecessarily in the wake of 'improvements' to the city's streets and roads. Today, the society still enjoys an active membership and is not only about the past; it is also concerned with the future shape and look of Norwich and promotes good design in new architecture and planning.

N.O.R.W.I.C.H.

A number of postal acronyms were first used during the Second World War to convey messages between servicemen and their wives or sweethearts. These included S.W.A.L.K. (Sealed With A Loving Kiss) and B.U.R.M.A. (Be Undressed Ready My Angel) as well as one for our beloved city – N.O.R.W.I.C.H. which suggested ((k)Nickers Off Ready When I Come Home).

VISCOUNT NORWICH

In 1952, Conservative Party politician and author Alfred Duff Cooper (1890–1954) was created Viscount Norwich, of Aldwick in the County of Sussex, in recognition of his political and literary career. His son, John Julius Cooper, 2nd Viscount Norwich, is well known as the historian, travel writer, broadcaster and television personality John Julius Norwich.

COURTING COUPLES

In March 1966, an article in *The Times* reported that Norwich Castle Museum was welcoming courting couples who would pay the 6*d* entrance fee and snuggle in the dim corners of the Norfolk Room which displays animals and birds of the East Anglian countryside to do some 'necking'. Curator Mr Francis Cheetham commented that, 'It is one of our jobs to provide a public service. We ought to be proud that we are providing a quiet, warm room, out of the rain for courting couples. They are some of our best behaved visitors.'

IF YOU GREW UP IN NORWICH IN THE 1970s AND '80s YOU PROBABLY …

- Had your first 'grown up' hair cut at George Clapham's barbers on Magdalen Street.
- Remember the magic of a visit to Langley's toyshop.

- Got your bicycle fixed at Dodger's on Chapel Street.
- Got bored waiting for your mum in Snob fashion clothing shop.
- Were scared by the Egyptian mummy on display at the Castle Museum.
- Were fascinated by the talking mynah bird outside the pet shop on Bell Avenue (Cattle Market Hill) until you were dragged away by a parent after it came out with a less-than-appropriate word for young ears.
- Bought a pair of Sta-Press trousers at Mr Byrite on the Haymarket or a puffball skirt from Chelsea Girl.
- Had fresh jam doughnuts from Don Miller's.
- Purchased a fashionable pair of shoes from Freeman, Hardy and Willis.
- Enjoyed the aroma of Mackintosh's chocolate factory in the city air.
- Sat in a traffic tailback for hours when your folks took you to go and wade through mud at the Norfolk Show – and had an official day off from school to go!
- Went to Saturday Club at the ABC Cinema on Prince of Wales Road or at the Odeon, Anglia Square.
- Brought pick 'n' mix sweets from Woolworth's on Rampant Horse Street.
- Thought dinner at the Berni Inn on Tombland was a posh meal out.
- Went to see a panto at the Theatre Royal starring 'Benny' from Crossroads 'back by popular demand'.
- Had a burger from Zak's Diner when it was a portacabin near the Cattle Market.
- Bought an album on cassette tape from Andy's Records on Lower Goat Lane.
- Saw 'Marigold' direct traffic in his washing-up gloves.
- Danced on the illuminated floor at Hy's Nightclub on Tombland.

THE ONLY NURSERY RHYME TO MENTION NORWICH

The Man in the Moon

The man in the moon came tumbling down
And asked his way to Norwich;
He went by the south and burnt his mouth
With supping cold pease porridge.

NORWICH DIALECT

The Norwich dialect and accent is distinct and different to that of the rest of Norfolk. Words are often squashed together; for example, county folk will say 'Norrrwich Citeee', where as the Norwich man (and woman) will say 'Norch Citi'. Here are a few words and phrases from the native tongue of Norwich:

Aaar – An hour
Aar you gorn up thu' Pust Arrfuss – Are you going to the Post Office?
Ass roit gud onya – That is really good of you
Ass a rum ol' jarb – That is a tricky or strange situation
Ass on the skoo – It is not straight
Buth arnum – Both of them
Carra Rud – Carrow Road (the ground where Norwich City Football Club play)
Dew yew lissen hare – Pay attention
Dornt – Don't
Ee gitonya narves – I get fed up with him
Fast clarss – First class
Git arf – Get off
Gorn up citi ta doo a bi' a shaarpen – Going to the city to do some shopping
Gretole – A large thing
Hayya gotta bead on? – Are you working hard or sweating?
Hiz hedda foo – That man is drunk
Hant – Have not
Hayya? – Have you?
Intut? – Isn't it?
Oi gaat rong – I got in trouble, argued or was told off
Oi hatta larf – It was funny
Stare-shun – Where trains arrive and depart
Suffun – Something
Thank ya my bewty – Thank you my friend
Werra much – Very much
Wuh? – An exclamation or query

14

ON
THIS DAY

JANUARY

1 January 1931 Norwich motor police patrols commence operations under the new Road Traffic Act.

2 January 1929 Cathedral authorities decide to install Marconiphone amplifiers in the nave.

4 January 1952 A huge fire in a four-storey building belonging to the Michelin Tyre Company on Lady's Lane destroyed 20,000 tyres and tubes valued at £25,000.

5 January 1923 Dr Bunnett died aged 88. He had been the city organist for many years.

6 January 1945 Norwich honoured the Royal Norfolk Regiment by granting it the freedom of the city and the privilege of marching through the city with colours flying, band playing and bayonets fixed.

7 January 1769 The church belonging to the Dutch congregation was used as a chapel for the poor of the workhouses for the first time.

8 January 1846 The last horse-drawn mail coach ran from Norwich to London.

10 January 1756 The shock of an earthquake was felt in Norwich.

12 January 1924 The bicentenary of the foundation of the Bethel Hospital.

14 January 1932 The new Cavell Mixed Primary School was opened on the Lakenham Estate.

16 January 1940 The Norwich City Air Training Corps Committee was formed.

17 January 1920 Princess Mary presided at a rally of 2,000 Norfolk Girl Guides at St Andrew's Hall, Norwich.

19 January 1876 The first 'spelling bee' to test the orthographical and philological knowledge of the competitors in Norwich was held at Noverre's Rooms, Norwich.

20 January 1923 The first case tried before only female magistrates was held at Norwich Guildhall.

25 January 1920 General Lord Horne unveiled the war memorial window at St Barnabas, Heigham.

26 January 1927 Telephone service between USA and Norfolk opened and the first messages were transmitted.

28 January 1809 Norwich flooded as the result of a rapid thaw of frost and heavy snowfall. Some houses were under 6 or 7ft of water and boats were rowed up St Martin's at Oak Street.

29 January 1883 The first of the touring pantomime companies appeared at Norwich Theatre: Messrs Sheridan and Watkins put on *Little Red Riding Hood*, originally produced at Yarmouth Theatre.

31 January 1756 One of the first provincial banks was established in Norwich under the direction of Charles Weston.

FEBRUARY

1 February 1932 The Carleton Cinema on All Saints Green was opened by Mr H. Frazer, the Sheriff of Norwich.

2 February 1921 King George V, the queen and Princess Mary visited Norwich and inspected works in progress for unemployed relief and housing.

7 February 1940 Stained glass from the Guildhall east window was removed for safety amid fears of it being damaged if Norwich was bombed.

8 February 1923 A great fire occurred at Brett's furniture shop, Heigham Street.

9 February 1921 Some 1,200 unemployed men mustered in Norwich Market Place to protest for outdoor relief on an increased scale or for the provision of schemes of work. Marching behind a red flag, they approached the workhouse where a scuffle broke out, three men were arrested and PC Pink was knocked unconscious.

10 February 1910 Explorer Sir Ernest Shackleton gave a lecture at St Andrew's Hall.

11 February 1888 Notorious Norfolk poacher Robert Large and George Annison were the first prisoners to escape from the new HM Prison Norwich. Both were later recaptured.

12 February 1936 An explosion on Trinity Street destroyed one house and damaged two others.

13 February 1936 The lady mayoress opened the extension to Hellesdon Mental Hospital Nurses Home.

17 February 1936 A fire on St Stephen's Street puts itself out by melting a water pipe.

18 February 1911 The Picture House Cinematograph Theatre opened on the Haymarket.

19 February 1925 The new Whitefriar's Bridge was opened for pedestrian traffic.

20 February 1963 Two shops, a confectioners and a horticulturalists had to be abandoned in Golden Ball Street because of subsidence.

21 February 1879 Edward Payson Weston, the American pedestrian, passed through Norwich on his walk of 2,000 miles in 1,000 consecutive hours (excluding Sundays).

24 February 1879 A descriptive lecture was given at St Andrew's Hall on the possibilities of the electric light, under the auspices of the Anglo-American Electric Lighting Company Limited by Mr H. Edmunds, a representative of the company.

25 February 1898 Norwegian Arctic explorer Dr Fridtjof Nansen delivered his lecture entitled 'Across the Polar Region' at St Andrew's Hall.

28 February 1934 The Bracondale and Trowse tram to Orford Place made its last journey.

MARCH

1 March 1836 The new police were on duty for the first time in Norwich.

2 March 1888 Jem Mace, 'retired champion of the world', appeared at Norwich Theatre in a series of exhibition sparring contests with Wolf Bendoff, Pooley Mace and Mike Jennett.

3 March 1988 The No. 26 double-decker bus to Hellesdon was travelling along Earlham Road when a hole opened up and the back end of the bus fell into it.

5 March 1926 A great fire occurred at Messrs Williams' Cabinet Works, St Paul's. The factory and three cottages were burnt out.

10 March 1952 A Colorado beetle was found in an imported lettuce in Norwich.

12 March 1916 Cringleford Mill was destroyed by fire.

13 March 1976 The Roman Catholic church of St John the Baptist was granted cathedral status by the Vatican.

14 March 1927 The Round Table was founded by Eminio William Louis Marchesi at Suckling House, Norwich.

18 March 1913 Lord Mayor Mr A.M. Samuel presented the city with a chain and pendants for the use of each lady mayoress.

21 March 1897 Mark Knights, antiquarian, author of *Highways and Byways of Norwich* and chief reporter of the *Eastern Daily Press* died on this day.

24 March 1937 A new bus station opened on Surrey Street, Norwich.

25 March 1937 Some 3,000 women took part in the Cathedral for Mothers' Union Festival at Norwich Cathedral.

27 March 1929 Blyth Secondary School for Girls opened at New Catton.

29 March 1867 Charles Dickens appeared at St Andrew's Hall, Norwich, where he read *Dr Marigold* and the trial scene from *The Pickwick Papers* before a large audience.

31 March 1908 The Cock public house at Old Lakenham was gutted by a fire.

APRIL

1 April 1923 Mrs W. Carey, wife of a Norwich tailor, gave birth to triplets – all girls.

2 April 1935 Opening of the Norwich–Leicester–Bristol Air Service.

4 April 1817 The boiler of Wright's Norwich and Yarmouth Steam Packet exploded just after starting out from Foundry Bridge. Five men, three women and one child was killed, and a further six women were left with fractured legs and arms, one of whom died in hospital.

8 April 1896 Arctic explorer and navigator Captain Wiggins, who had recently returned from Siberia, lectured in Norwich upon the Nansen expedition.

9 April 1910 Theatre de Luxe cinematograph show opened on St Andrew Street.

10 April 1862 Jenny Lind appeared at a concert given at St Andrew's Hall, Norwich.

11 April 1975 Queen Elizabeth II paid an official visit to Norwich.

12 April 1995 The Assembly House in Norwich burnt out but was restored in a £385,000 project.

13 April 1883 A specially invited company visited Carrow Works to witness the lighting of the premises for the first time with the electric light installed by the Hammond Electric Light and Power Supply Company.

15 April 1830 In one of the last public whippings in Norfolk, William King was whipped in Norwich Market Place for stealing a pewter pot.

18 April 1935 Swimming pool opened at Samson and Hercules House.

19 April 1968 Fire destroyed part of the administration block at the Norfolk and Norwich Hospital.

20 April 1960 The University Grants Committee approved the plan to establish a university in Norwich.

```
"THE  CENTRE  OF  NORFOLK."
Samson  &  Hercules  House
TOMBLAND,  NORWICH  (Telephone  922)
          Opposite the Cathedral

        MAGNIFICENT  MODERN
    SWIMMING        POOL
    Open EVERY DAY during the Summer Season

    SPACIOUS    BALLROOM
    WITH  LUXURIOUS  SURROUNDINGS  -  CABARET  SHOWS
          PERMANENT  DANCE  ORCHESTRA
    (The Ballroom is available for hire during the winter months)

            VISIT  THE
    15TH  CENTURY  CAFE- RESTAURANT
    Open from 9 a.m. to 10.30 p.m. ALL THE YEAR ROUND FOR LUNCHEONS,
            TEAS, DINNERS, LIGHT REFRESHMENTS

    15th CENTURY SURROUNDINGS  -  20th CENTURY SERVICE

    PRIVATE  ROOMS for Meetings, Dinners, Receptions, etc.
```

22 April 1995 Eighth National Juggling Competition was hosted in Norwich.

23 April 1910 A military tournament by the 16th Lancers took place at the Agricultural Hall.

24 April 1648 The biggest explosion during the English Civil War occurred in Norwich on Monday, 24 April 1648, when the armoury in the country committee headquarters house near St Peter Mancroft church blew up.

25 April 1934 The new Thorpe Hamlet Senior Girls' School was opened by the Lord Mayor.

26 April 1889 The phonograph, described as Edison's wonderful talking machine, was exhibited for the first time in Norwich, 'with a unique library of voices', by Mr William Lynd.

27 April 1942 The first night of the Baedeker Blitz on Norwich saw 50 tons of bombs dropped, 162 killed, and 600 injured.

29 April 1942 The second night of the Baedeker Blitz saw 45 tons of high explosive and thousands of incendiaries dropped on Norwich. There were sixty-nine people killed and eighty-nine seriously injured.

30 April 1932 The Municipal Golf Course was opened at Earlham.

MAY

1 May 1930 United double-decker buses started running from Catton Grove to Thorpe.

2 May 1785 Schools were opened to instruct the charity boys in Norwich in the art of spinning.

3 May 1932 Prince George attended the consecration of the War Memorial Chapel at Norwich Cathedral.

4 May 1926 The General Strike commenced in Norwich.

5 May 1740 The weather was so cold that snow fell at 10 a.m. and hung on the cathedral spire.

6 May 1935 King George V Jubilee celebrations in the city.

7 May 1914 Viscount Coke presented the colours to Norwich Cathedral Troop of Scouts.

8 May 1945 VE Day celebrations saw 5,000 people march through the streets of Norwich to the service at the cathedral.

10 May 1820 Oil gas lamps were lit in Norwich Market Place and adjoining streets for the first time.

12 May 1926 The General Strike was declared 'off'.

14 May 1929 Mile Cross Gardens were officially opened.

15 May 1919 Nurse Cavell's body was interred at Life's Green after due ceremony.

16 May 1930 An explosion occurred near Thorpe Station and a manhole cover was blown up.

17 May 1921 Sir Eustace Gurney presented Lazar House, Sprowston, to the city.

18 May 1935 The London and North Easter Railway ran their first evening excursion to London at a price of 4*s*.

19 May 1995 Tibetan monks visit Norwich.

21 May 1780 Elizabeth Fry (née Gurney), prison and social reformer, Quaker and Christian philanthropist, was born in Gurney Court off Magdalen Street.

25 May 1900 Architect George Skipper's masterpiece, the Royal Arcade Hotel, was opened for the first time. It was built on the site of the old Royal Hotel, hence its 'Royal' appellation.

26 May 1966 The 400-year-old 10cwt bronze bell from St Etheldreda's church belfry was stolen.

29 May 1929 Harry Moulton, the last Norwich bellman, died on this day at the age of 73.

30 May 1928 The Prince of Wales opened Eaton Park.

31 May 1976 The Radio One Roadshow came to the Norwich Spring Bank Holiday Fete on Earlham Park.

JUNE

1 June 1934 Norwich Lido opened on Aylsham Road.

2 June 1925 Prince Henry (Duke of Gloucester) opened the new Lad's Club in the city.

4 June 1931 A new branch library opened at Mile Cross.

7 June 1911 The formal opening of the new golf links at Eaton.

10 June 1809 Dr John Beckwith, eminent musician, composer and organist at Norwich Cathedral, died aged 49.

11 June 1931 New swimming pool opened at Roxley Road, Thorpe St Andrew.

12 June 1962 A French two-tone air horn was tried out on one of the Norwich Fire Brigade engines as the bells used to date were finding too much competition among modern traffic noise.

13 June 1802 Author Harriet Martineau was born in Norwich.

14 June 1814 The Norfolk Lunatic Asylum at Thorpe opened for the reception of patients.

19 June 1842 A severe thunderstorm occurred at Norwich. The wind blew a perfect hurricane, rushing in a straight line for Catton where it caught the high wall in St Clement's Square and blew down about 30yds of solid brickwork. The sails of Catton mill were blown off, trees were torn up by their roots and the river suddenly rose above the banks in places.

20 June 1914 A County Scout Rally was held at Crown Point with an inspection by 'B-P' himself – Sir Robert Baden-Powell.

21 June 1898 The Norwich Corporation Baths opened on St Andrew's Street.

22 June 1934 The Theatre Royal burnt down on this day.

23 June 1937 St Peter Hungate Museum of Ecclesiastical Art was opened by the Lord Mayor.

24 June 1912 The formal dedication of the sea cadet training ship *Lord Nelson*.

25 June 1960 The last cattle market was held on the Cattle Market near the castle.

27 June 1923 Edward, Prince of Wales opened the new Carrow Bridge.

28 June 1853 Spiritualism was introduced to Norwich when the first séance was held at St Andrew's Hall by Mr King.

29 June 1930 A pathway on Earlham Road subsided, leaving a 20ft-deep hole.

30 June 1883 Norwich experienced a disastrous thunderstorm and several low-lying streets were flooded. A man was killed when he was struck by lightning near Unthank Road and another suffered the same fate at Earlham.

JULY

1 July 1814 A well-attended public meeting at St Andrew's Hall resolved support for the petition to both Houses of Parliament for the abolition of the African Slave Trade.

2 July 1960 The new Norwich Cattle Market at Harford Bridge was opened for its first day of business after the previous day's official opening by Alderman Herbert Frazer, chairman of the market's committee.

3 July 1932 The Graf Zeppelin airship passed over Norwich for the first time on her trip round Great Britain.

4 July 1912 The dedication of the new organ at St Peter Mancroft.

5 July 1936 Sir Oswald Moseley addressed a Fascist meeting in the Market Place.

6 July 1929 Old Jenny Lind Children's Infirmary buildings in Pottergate Street were closed and the outpatients department removed to Eaton.

7 July 1924 Costessey Flour Mills burnt down with £10,000 damage.

8 July 1931 The new Eastern Counties bus terminus was opened in Thorpe Station Yard.

9 July 1940 The City of Norwich suffered its first air raid of the war.

10 July 1927 The first solo flight for Norfolk and Norwich Aero Club was made on Mousehold by Mr W. Moore of Great Yarmouth.

11 July 1772 The Norfolk and Norwich Hospital (erected by public subscription) first opened for outpatients.

12 July 1936 A woman has her clothes burnt off on Chapel Field Gardens and later died.

16 July 1887 The new prison, built to replace the Norwich Castle Prison and the old Norwich City Gaol, was opened on Prison Road (now Knox Road).

17 July 1936 The foundation stone of Norwich Christian Spiritualist church was laid.

18 July 1761 The *Norwich Gazette* newspaper was first printed by John Crouse.

19 July 1922 The James Stuart Memorial Garden on Recorder Road was formally handed over to the city.

22 July 1960 A whirlwind struck Taverham, throwing sheds at Gallant's Farm in the air and killed fifty turkeys.

25 July 1995 Closed-circuit TV cameras observing the streets of Norwich were switched on for the first time.

26 July 1922 The foundation stones of Regent Theatre on Prince of Wales Road were laid by the Lord Mayor and sheriff.

27 July 1929 Lord Mayor H.P. Gowen laid the foundation stone for the parish hall and St Anne's church, Earlham.

29 July 1899 Barnum & Bailey Circus – 'The Greatest Show on Earth' – came to Norwich.

30 July 1932 The new Norwich Coaching Station was opened on Castle Meadow.

AUGUST

1 August 1994 Norwich Central Library caught fire and extensive damage was caused.

5 August 1865 A large meeting of agriculturists was held at the Swan Hotel, Norwich, for the purpose of considering what steps should be taken to combat a disease known as the Russian murrain, which had broken out among the cattle of Norfolk.

6 August 1889 The Royal Archaeological Institute of Great Britain and Ireland visited Norwich and held its inaugural meeting at St Andrew's Hall.

7 August 1971 The final closure of Norwich City Greyhound Stadium at Boundary Park, Hellesdon, was announced on this day.

9 August 1911 One of the hottest days on record in Norwich saw temperatures of 93.7 degrees.

10 August 1912 Bentfield C. Hucks became the first man to fly over Norwich in an aircraft.

11 August 1921 The Norfolk Regiment War Memorial Cottages in Norwich were formally inaugurated by the Earl of Leicester.

12 August 1921 A memorial to six Norfolk county cricketers who fell in the First World War was unveiled at the county ground at Lakenham during the interval of the second-class county match between Norfolk and Bedfordshire.

13 August 1930 Archbishops, bishops and East Anglian mayors attended a commemoration service at the cathedral for the 1,300th anniversary of the diocese.

15 August 1945 VJ Day celebrations took place across Norfolk, rejoicing in the end of the war in the Far East, where many Norfolk men were serving or enduring captivity as prisoners of war in Japanese hands.

17 August 1850 Hannah Sarah Hancock, born at St Helen's in Norwich in 1781, died on this day. She compiled a dictionary for children when she was just 8 years old.

18 August 1936 Mr E. Barclay of Colney Hall made a gift of a covered stand to Norwich City Football Club.

19 August 1960 Norwich recovered after the previous day's torrential rain fall, measured at 1in in less than an hour, which caused a landslide on to the mainline to London at Trowse. In Norwich itself, two roads subsided, while shops, offices and even the City Hall were flooded.

20 August 1842 Completion of the refacing of Norwich Castle in Bath stone after the original walls had fallen into a bad state of repair.

22 August 1924 St Faith's Abbey was struck by lightning and burnt down.

23 August 1965 A skeleton dug up in the garden of River View Bungalow in Hellesdon on this day was believed to be that of a man killed during Kett's Rebellion in 1549.

24 August 1936 Gracie Fields appeared at the Theatre Royal.

26 August 1912 The first of three days when Norwich suffered severe flooding. Over 750 acres and 3,650 buildings, including thirty-three churches and fifty-nine factories, were affected by the floodwaters.

29 August 1959 Following amalgamation with the Suffolk Regiment, the regimental flag of the Royal Norfolk Regiment was lowered for the last time at Britannia Barracks, Norwich.

30 August 1881 The Norwich Town Council, who had erected two electric lights in the Market Place, decided to extend the system experimentally to several of the principal streets, at a cost not exceeding £400, for twelve months.

31 August 1935 Norwich City Football Club's new football ground was opened on Carrow Road by Mr Russell Colman, Lord Lieutenant of Norfolk.

SEPTEMBER

1 September 1908 The first match was played at The Nest, the first purpose-built home ground for Norwich City Football Club.

5 September 1936 New Christian Spiritualist church opened on Chapel Field North.

6 September 1935 Norwich City Council erected the first Belisha beacons in the city.

7 September 1931 The first cinema organ in Norwich was installed at the Haymarket Picture House.

8 September 1910 The City of Norwich School, Eaton, was opened by the Revd Hon. Edward Lyttelton, headmaster of Eton.

9 September 1925 The official opening of Wensum Park (formerly a refuse tip) by the Lord Mayor, Dr G.S. Pope.

10 September 1874 The Thorpe Railway Disaster. Two trains collided head-on at Thorpe St Andrew. Both drivers and firemen were killed, as were seventeen passengers with four later dying from their injuries.

11 September 1924 The new Blue Bell Road was opened by the Lord Mayor, Miss E.M. Colman.

12 September 1923 The formal opening of the new Mile Cross Road by Sir Henry P. Maybury.

13 September 1930 The five-minute bell at Thorpe Station was rung for the last time.

14 September 1885 The first exhibition by members of the Norwich Art Circle (formed in the month of February) was opened at the Old Bank of England Chambers, Queen Street.

16 September 1878 Many of the streets in the low-lying areas of the city were flooded, and hundreds of the inhabitants were compelled to leave their houses by means of boats. An enormous amount of distress prevailed.

19 September 1940 Displays of the aurora borealis were seen over the city.

23 September 1936 Sir Thomas Beecham conducted on the opening night of the Triennial Musical Festival. A 'brilliant' first night.

24 September 1940 The 1,000lb bomb that landed on Theatre Street a week earlier was defused and removed by a brave team of Royal Engineers.

26 September 1921 Maddermarket Theatre was opened with a performance of *As You Like It* by the Norwich Players.

27 September 1988 The first superloo in Norfolk was opened on Redwell Street.

30 September 1935 New Theatre Royal opened with a performance of *White Horse Inn*.

OCTOBER

5 October 1959 The first edition of BBC *Look East* was aired.

9 October 1927 Norwich War Memorial was unveiled by Bertie Withers, a private soldier who had been severely wounded at the Battle of Gaza while serving with 4th Battalion, The Norfolk Regiment.

10 October 1900 The Time Ball atop Norwich Castle was fired for the first time.

11 October 1859 Charles Dickens gave a selection of readings from *A Christmas Carol* and *The Pickwick Papers* at St Andrew's Hall, Norwich.

12 October 1940 Clement Attlee, Lord Privy Seal, visited Norwich and placed a wreath on Nurse Cavell's grave on the 25th anniversary of her martyrdom.

14 October 1963 Millions of Christmas crackers exploded when a fire broke out in a Norwich factory store.

15 October 1932 Queen Elizabeth opened the Queen Alexandra Nurses' Home at the Norfolk and Norwich Hospital.

16 October 1924 Magdalen Road caved in at the junction with Knowsley Road.

17 October 1963 The freedom of Norwich was conferred on the 1st East Anglian Regiment. More than 300 officers and men paraded through the city with fixed bayonets.

19 October 1905 The statue of the great Norwich scholar Sir Thomas Browne was unveiled by Lord Avebury.

21 October 1805 Admiral Nelson died shortly after learning of his victory at the Battle of Trafalgar.

22 October 1751 The Bridewell was gutted by fire.

23 October 1894 The Duke and Duchess of York visited Norwich and opened the Castle Museum and Art Gallery.

24 October 1925 The Duke of York opened the Bridewell Museum of Local Industries on Bridewell Alley.

25 October 1909 King Edward VII paid what was to be his last official visit to Norwich.

27 October 1762 A sudden flood hit the city, leaving 300 houses and eight parish churches under water.

28 October 1838 The first meeting of the Chartist movement in Norfolk was held on this day in Norwich Market Place.

29 October 1938 The new Norwich City Hall is opened by King George VI and Queen Elizabeth.

30 October 1910 General Baden Powell visited the Boy Scouts at the Drill Hall, Norwich.

NOVEMBER

1 November 1929 The R101 airship passed over Norwich on her trial flight.

3 November 1860 A description was published of an iron lighthouse, completed by Messrs Barnard, Bishop and Barnard of the Norfolk Ironworks, Norwich, for the Brazilian Government.

5 November 1962 £1,300 in banknotes, savings certificates and a post office savings account book fell out of an armchair that was being lifted on to a Norwich bonfire. The stash was identified as that of former bus conductor Frank Duggan who had died earlier that year and the chair had been discarded when his property had been cleared.

6 November 1794 A sudden flood hit Norwich causing great distress to the poor inhabitants of Heigham and other low-lying parts of the city. Boats were rowed in several streets and the water was 2ft or 3ft deep in many houses.

9 November 1923 Miss Ethel Colman was appointed the first lady Lord Mayor of Norwich.

10 November 1925 The coke heap at Norwich Gas Works was found on fire. It burned for over a week.

12 November 1936 New Church at Mile Cross was consecrated by the Bishop of Norwich.

15 November 1899 The Norwich Omnibus Company (formed in 1878) wound up its affairs in consequence of the approaching completion of the tramways scheme.

16 November 1965 Eight American Congressman and three of their staff reviewed the electronic postal code system at the GPO Norwich sorting office.

19 November 1770 Norwich suffered a severe flood.

22 November 2007 1st Battalion, the Royal Anglian Regiment, were greeted with a heroes' return after an intense six-month deployment in Helmand Province, Afghanistan.

25 November 1998 The new Norwich Crown Court was officially opened.

26 November 1863 Brother Ignatius, a clergyman of the English Church, who 'had the temerity to come before a public audience attired as a Benedictine monk' with bare head and bare feet, carrying a rosary and crucifix, lectured at St Andrew's Hall on 'Monks and Monasteries for the English Church'.

29 November 1921 Earl Haig visited the Norfolk County Asylum at Thorpe to unveil a plaque to mark its role as the Norfolk War Hospital; it provided over 2,000 beds for wounded servicemen during the First World War.

30 November 1875 St Andrew's Day was celebrated in Norwich by the members of the newly formed St Andrew Society dining at the Maid's Head Hotel. Mr T. Muir Grant, the founder and president of the society, was in the chair and Dr Waddell, the vice-president, officiated as croupier.

DECEMBER

1 December 1980 The opening night of the Norwich Puppet Theatre saw a performance of *Humbug, Humbug*, an interpretation of Dickens' *A Christmas Carol*.

3 December 1923 The new Regent Theatre on Prince of Wales Road was formally opened.

7 December 1549 Robert Kett, the leader of the Norfolk rebellion, was executed and gibbeted upon the walls of Norwich Castle.

8 December 1910 The Roman Catholic church of St John the Baptist (now the Roman Catholic cathedral) was opened with solemn ceremonial.

10 December 1935 The last tram service ran in Norwich.

13 December 1980 An anti-nuclear protest marched from in front of City Hall to Bawburgh underground government shelter.

15 December 1954 1st Battalion, the Royal Norfolk Regiment was given a civic welcome in Norwich after the soldiers' return from The Korean War.

16 December 1843 The improvement of Briggs' Street, Norwich, was completed and the Paving Commissioners were paid £700.

17 December 1940 Postwomen, last seen during the First World War, reappear on the streets of Norwich.

19 December 1924 The Hawthornden Prize for the best novel of the year was presented to Norwich author R.H. Mottram for *The Spanish Farm*.

20 December 1921 Strangers' Hall and its contents were presented to the city by Mr L.G. Bolingbroke.

23 December 1954 The clubhouse and all the racing craft of the Norwich Amateur Rowing Association at Whitlingham were destroyed in a fire.

25 December 1860 This was the coldest Christmas that had been experienced for at least a century. At the Literary Institute at Norwich, the minimum registered was 3 degrees above zero. At Costessey, the register was 7 degrees below zero, or 39 degrees lower than the point at which water freezes. The ice was about 4in thick.

26 December 1856 Boxing Day was observed in Norwich as a general holiday for the first time.

27 December 1925 A house in Baker's Yard, Barrack Street, in which twenty-two people resided, collapsed without injury to anyone.

31 December 1808 Boxing legends John Gulley, Tom Cribb and Tom Belcher gave a boxing exhibition at Norwich before an audience of 800 people.

ABOUT THE AUTHOR

NEIL R. STOREY is a born and bred Norfolk man and glories in being so. He has written over twenty-five books and numerous articles about the city and county he knows and loves so well. Some of his other works include *The Little Book of Norfolk*, *The Little Book of Great Britain*, *The Little Book of Death* and *The Little Book of Murder*.

BIBLIOGRAPHY

BOOKS

Anderson, A.P. and Storey, Neil R., *Eighty Years of the Norwich Society* (Sutton, 2004)

Atkin, Malcolm, *Norwich: History and Guide* (Stroud, 1993)

Brookes, Pamela, *Norfolk Miscellany* (Derby, 2009)

Browne, Philip, *The History of Norwich* (Norwich, 1814)

Cluer, Andrew and Shaw, Michael, *Former Norwich* (Attleborough, 1972)

Cotman, Alec M. and Hawcroft, Francis W., *Old Norwich* (Norwich, 1961)

Davis, Anthony (ed.), *Anglia Television: The First Twenty-One Years* (Norwich, 1980)

Daynes, J., *The History of Norwich* (Norwich, 1848)

Dew, Walton N., *A Dyshe of Norfolke Dumplings* (London, 1898)

Forby, Robert, *The Vocabulary of East Anglia* (London, 1830)

Glyde, John, *The Norfolk Garland* (London, 1872)

Hudson, Revd William and Tingey, John Cottingham, *The Records of the City of Norwich* (Norwich, 1906)

Kent, Arnold and Stephenson, Andrew, *Norwich Inheritance* (Norwich, 1948)

Knights, Mark, *The Highways and Byeways of Old Norwich* (Norwich, 1887)

Mackie, Charles, *Norfolk Annals*, 2 vols (Norwich, 1901)

Mardle, Jonathan (foreword by), *Broad Norfolk* (Norwich, 1949)

Matchett, J. (ed.), *The Norfolk and Norwich Remembrancer and Vade-Mecum* (Norwich, 1822)

Mee, Arthur, *The King's England: Norfolk* (London, 1940)

Nobbs, George, *Norwich: A City of Centuries* (Norwich, 1971)

Nobbs, George, *Norwich City Hall* (Norwich, 1988)

Ogley, Bob; Davisdon, Mark; and Currie, Ian, *The Norfolk and Suffolk Weather Book* (Westerham, 1993)

Plunkett, George A.F., *Rambles in Old Norwich* (Lavenham, 1990)

Rawcliffe, Carole and Wilson, Richard (eds), *Medieval Norwich* (London, 2004)

Rawcliffe, Carole and Wilson, Richard (eds), *Norwich Since 1550* (London, 2004)

Roberts, C.V. and Frankl, Ernest, *Norwich* (Cambridge, 1989)

Rye, Walter, *A History of Norfolk* (London, 1885)

Rye, Walter, *Tourist's Guide to Norfolk* (London, 1892)

Skipper, Keith, *Hidden Norfolk* (Newbury, 1998)

Skipper, Keith, *The Norfolk Connection* (Cromer, 1991)

Storey, Neil R., *A Century of Norwich* (Sutton, 2000)

Storey, Neil R., *A Norfolk Century* (Sutton, 1999)

Storey, Neil R., *Around Norwich* (Sutton, 1996)

Storey, Neil R., *Hanged at Norwich*, (Stroud, 2011)

Storey, Neil R., *Norfolk Floods* (Wellington, 2012)

Storey, Neil R., *Norfolk Goes to War* (Wellington, 2014)

Storey, Neil R., *Norwich – The Changing City* (Barnsley, 2002)

Thompson, Leonard P., *Norwich Inns* (Ipswich, 1947)

Wicks, Walter, *Inns and Taverns of Old Norwich* (Norwich, 1925)

Young, John Riddington, *The Inns and Taverns of Old Norwich* (Norwich, 1975)

Blyth's Norwich Guide and Directory
Kelly's Directory of Norfolk
Kelly's Directory of Norwich
The Norwich Almanac
White's Directory of Norfolk

NEWSPAPERS AND JOURNALS

East Anglian Magazine
Eastern Daily Press
Eastern Evening News
Norfolk Chronicle
Norfolk Fair
Norwich Mercury
The Times
The Observer

Also from The History Press

BLOODY BRITISH HISTORY

Britain has centuries of incredible history to draw on – everything from Boudica and the Black Death to the Blitz. This local series, harking back to the extraordinary pulp magazines of days gone by, contains only the darkest and most dreadful events in your area's history. So embrace the nastier side of British history with these tales of riots and executions, battles and sieges, murders and regicides, witches and ghosts, death, devilry and destruction!

Find these titles and more at
www.thehistorypress.co.uk

Also from The History Press

WHEN DISASTER STRIKES